The Fighting Scots

|The Fighting Scots|

of Edinboro

One Small School's Rise to Prominence Among College Wrestling's Heavyweights

by John Dudley

REEDY PRESS
St. Louis, Missouri

To E.T.D.
THE BEST TRAINING PARTNER A WRESTLING WRITER COULD HAVE

Library of Congress Control Number: 2008934219

ISBN: 978-1-933370-72-9

Please visit our website at www.reedypress.com.

Printed in the United States of America
08 09 10 11 12 5 4 3 2 1

Contents

Acknowledgments   vi

Foreword by Bruce Baumgartner   vii

Chapter One   Big Time   1

Chapter Two   "Iowa of the East"   12

Chapter Three   First Steps   21

Chapter Four   Baptisms   32

Chapter Five   Early Returns   40

Chapter Six   Success and All

                        Its Trimmings   53

Chapter Seven   O'Day   63

Chapter Eight   Transitions   73

Chapter Nine   Koscheck   85

Chapter Ten   Gillespie   98

Appendix   All-Time Roster   113
About the Author   118

Acknowledgments

THIS BOOK CAME CLOSE TO NOT HAPPENING MANY TIMES. FROM the beginning, Josh Stevens, co-partner at Reedy Press, saw the potential in a story about a small school competing among giants. Later, publisher Matt Heidenry put his blind faith in a first-time author and pushed it through to completion. I am indebted to both for their patience and their belief in the project.

My dear friend and former college professor Bill Schopf read and edited with a keen eye and a deft touch, all at the cost of a few decent lunches.

Bruce Baumgartner and Mike DeAnna graciously gave their time and assistance in re-creating the early years. Tim Flynn opened his program and gave me complete access to his wrestlers, never once questioning a request.

Former and current wrestlers, including Mike Hahesy, Sean O'Day, Tony Robie, Josh Koscheck, Jason Robison, and Gregor Gillespie, let me into their lives and patiently re-told the stories of their careers, sometimes in painful detail.

Also: Bob Shreve, Jim McDonald, Todd Jay, Lou Rosselli, Gary Astorino, Cliff Moore, and Fred Caro. To each, I am grateful.

To my family, including mom and dad, Leroy and Mildred and Doug and Abby, who offered encouragement at precisely the right times, sometimes unwittingly, and listened to many more wrestling stories than anyone should ever have to endure.

This book is lovingly dedicated to Ellen Dudley, Austin Dudley, Logan Dudley, and Megan Dudley for their almost limitless patience and unswerving support. You are my champions.

Foreword

THE EDINBORO UNIVERSITY WRESTLING PROGRAM HAS BEEN IN existence for over sixty-five years. During that time, the program has had 11 coaches, over 320 wrestlers, and numerous presidents and athletic directors. In the early 1980s, the decision was made to elevate the Division II wrestling program to Division I, which transformed Edinboro University wrestling into a nationally respected wrestling program. The transformation was a result of many events and individuals, but over the past twenty years, the Edinboro University wrestling program has grown to, and has maintained, national prominence.

In the college wrestling world, Edinboro University is greatly respected for its wrestling success. People are amazed that a state university of seventy-five hundred students that is NCAA Division II in all other sports can continually produce the consistent success in wrestling that it enjoys. Edinboro University has enjoyed wrestling wins over Division I programs like Arizona State, Illinois, Lehigh, Maryland, Michigan State, Missouri, North Carolina, Ohio State, Penn State, Pittsburgh, Stanford, Virginia Tech, West Virginia, and Wisconsin. An impressive group of major universities have been beaten by a small school that, in the college wrestling world, is now considered one of the "big boys."

Not all of that respect came easily, though. In the early years, several rival coaches from throughout the Pennsylvania State Athletic Conference (PSAC) dismissed Edinboro's chances for success at the Division I level, predicting that the program would never win a PSAC title. (The Fighting Scots have won the PSAC championship eleven times since moving to Division I in 1986, including nine of the past eleven.) Later, after Edinboro joined the Eastern Wrestling League (EWL), its new EWL rivals doubted the Scots could become one of the league's elite programs. (Edinboro has won ten EWL regular-season titles and ten tournament titles, including the past four.)

How can Edinboro wrestling continue to compete with the major Division I universities? The people behind the program are essential. From the president and director of athletics that elevated the program in the 1980s to current coach Tim Flynn, the program has been blessed with outstanding individuals that have special characteristics that led to the success of the program. Former athletic director James K. McDonald, an outstanding basketball player and coach, possessed a passion for success and an obsession to be the best that helped establish the foundation for the program's future success. Edinboro's first Division I coach, Mike DeAnna, a great high school wrestler in Ohio and collegiate wrestler at Iowa University, possessed a tunnel vision for wrestling and established an Iowa-like work ethic at Edinboro. Mike was so focused that at times it seemed his only interest in life was wrestling. Again, his initial leadership and his ability to recruit set the groundwork for instant and prolonged success.

DeAnna was responsible for recruiting individuals like Sean O'Day, a unique personality himself, and Mike Hahesy, an intriguing transfer from Iowa. Sean was a local state champion wrestler from Meadville High School who became Edinboro University's first NCAA Division I champion. His success helped solidify Edinboro's credibility as a Division I wrestling program and a local wrestling powerhouse. DeAnna and Hahesy brought the "Iowa" wrestling mystique to Edinboro that still continues today.

When Tim Flynn came to Edinboro University in the early 1990s, the program took another major step in the right direction. Tim's focus and passion for the sport is unsurpassed. His energy, work ethic, and knowledge of the sport are the major reasons that the program continues to be successful. Tim has surrounded himself with great wrestling recruits, the likes of Josh Koscheck, Edinboro's second NCAA champion and now a mixed martial arts fighter, and Gregor Gillespie, Edinboro's third NCAA champion.

Both have helped carry on an Edinboro tradition of champion wrestlers with fascinating personalities.

The individuals involved in the Edinboro wrestling program have continued to strive not only to maintain success, but to increase success each year. Even in recent years, the Scots have continued to record milestones. In 2006, Gregor Gillespie became the program's first true freshman to earn All-American honors at the national tournament. The following year, he became the first sophomore NCAA champion in the program's history. In 2008, Edinboro took ten qualifiers to the Division I nationals for the first time in the program's history. Gillespie entered the 2008–09 season with the opportunity to become the school's first repeat champ.

The passion to always improve is a major theme in the program. Success grows success. Some of Edinboro's most outstanding wrestlers have gone on to help build top programs elsewhere in the country. Tom Shiflett, a three-time All American in the early 1990s, has helped transform Hofstra into one of the nation's top programs. Lou Rosselli, a two-time All American who went on to represent Edinboro in the 1996 Olympic Games, is a top assistant at Ohio State, which has once again become an elite team.

Both Shiflett and Rosselli understand something that has always been an important part of the Edinboro philosophy—the better you do, the harder you have to work to improve. Where some programs hit a plateau and become complacent and even take a step back, Edinboro wrestling continues to push forward to reach for greater success, to continue to be the little school that can compete with the "big boys."

Bruce Baumgartner
April 2008

| Chapter One |

Big Time

GREGOR GILLESPIE'S FEET WERE NOWHERE NEAR THE GROUND. IN the center of a basketball arena outside Detroit, Gillespie had just reached the top of the college wrestling world, and he celebrated by leaping high into the air, arms outstretched, onto the shoulders of his coaches. Throughout most of the arena, which held more than 17,000 of the most passionate wrestling fans in the country, reactions ranged from polite applause to stunned silence. Many of the fans here on that night in March 2007 were from Michigan. They made the relatively short trip to the Palace of Auburn Hills, home of the NBA's Detroit Pistons, to watch a native son win an NCAA Division I wrestling title.

Josh Churella, a junior 149-pound wrestler for the University of Michigan, grew up in nearby Northville. His father, Mark, is a Michigan wrestling icon. He was a three-time NCAA champion regarded as Michigan's greatest wrestler ever. He was elected to the National Wrestling Hall of Fame. The Churellas' story made headlines in the local papers each day of the three-day national tournament. On this day—the final day, Saturday— the attention had reached its peak as Josh prepared for the national final and the chance to follow in his father's footsteps. Churella's opponent was Gillespie, who pulled off the biggest upset of Friday night's semifinal round by knocking off the top seed and defending champion, Dustin Schlatter of Minnesota, ending the nation's longest active winning streak. In spite of that win, Gillespie appeared to be the underdog. All week, television cameras and reporters circled Schlatter and Churella, two stars from richly-funded, universally respected Big Ten wrestling programs. Gillespie, meanwhile, went about his business mostly unnoticed, except for the occasional brief interview with a print reporter. As the Churella-Gillespie match approached, the fourth of ten national finals that would be wrestled at the Palace on this night and beamed live to a national television audience watching on ESPN, the big crowd began to stir. Seldom does a college wrestler get the chance to win a national title in his home state, much less thirty minutes from home. But Churella was on the verge of doing just that. All that stood between him and the picture-perfect moment in amateur sports was seven minutes of wrestling against a sophomore from a tiny school six hours away in the sleepy Pennsylvania countryside. It would have been hard to find anyone at the Palace that night who thought Gillespie had much of a chance, most of all Churella, whose respect for any opponent was far surpassed by the confidence any great athlete, particularly a wrestler, has in his ability to win any time in any place. The Michigan fans were waiting for the chance to explode. Many others in the crowd were expecting to see Churella dominate—especially those from the powerful programs of the Big Ten and Big 12 who through decades of dominating the college wrestling landscape had grown accustomed to winning match-ups like this one, and deservedly so. Very few of them had even entertained the possibility that Churella might lose. Gillespie, though, had no doubt he could win.

⚜   ⚜   ⚜   ⚜   ⚜

Twenty-three years earlier, on a crisp January night in a small college town about ninety miles north of Pittsburgh, the Edinboro Fighting Scots had just been handed a humiliating 57–0 home defeat by a familiar rival.

Clarion University is located only about an hour from Edinboro, but at that point its wrestling program was a universe apart from its longtime Pennsylvania State Athletic Conference (PSAC) opponent. The Golden Eagles had pumped money into their program for years, handing out scholarships and upgrading

Former coach Fred Caro, who compiled a 135-98-4 record in 22
seasons before Mike DeAnna's arrival in 1984.

facilities, and they arrived in Edinboro as the seventeenth ranked
Division I program in the country.

The PSAC was then, and is now, largely a conference of
state-owned, Division II sports-playing institutions. But several
conference schools had begun to upgrade their wrestling
programs with an eye toward moving to Division I. Making such
a jump in football would require, even at that time, an investment

of hundreds of thousands of dollars with no assurance of ever turning a profit. Wrestling, on the other hand, required no pads or helmets or blocking sleds. Coaching staffs were much smaller than those in most football programs, and rosters were a fraction of the size. Plus, Pennsylvania was rich in high school wrestling talent, meaning PSAC schools could save money on their recruiting budgets by scouting and signing talent close to home. In short, the jump to the highest level of collegiate wrestling was much easier to make than in many other sports.

At the time of the Clarion match, though, Edinboro had not yet made that jump. The Scots, under Coach Fred Caro, had a reputation as a scrappy, yet vastly under-funded program that lacked the resources and facilities to compete with its richer PSAC foes. Through neglect and indifference on the part of Edinboro's athletic officials, it was quickly falling behind schools like Clarion, Lock Haven, and Bloomsburg, all of whom had made significant investments in wrestling and were enjoying success both in the state and nationally. Every year it was becoming more of a challenge for Caro and his staff to convince wrestlers to come to Edinboro and compete. Everyone agreed it was not Caro's fault. Long respected in Pennsylvania wrestling circles, Caro had enjoyed plenty of success at Edinboro, even on the national level. He compiled a 135–98–4 record over twenty-two seasons, and in 1973 he coached an NAIA national champion, Tom Herr. Yet, the disparity between how Edinboro handled its wrestling program and how it handled other sports had become great. Winning required more than persistence and good coaching. It required miracles. By the mid-1980s, the school had begun fund-raising campaigns for several other sports, including football, men's and women's basketball, and cross country, but that money never reached wrestling. Wrestling was passing Edinboro by, and that became crystal clear on the night of January 25, 1984, when Clarion swept all ten weight classes—seven of them by scoring the maximum six team points by pin or forfeit—and then added one final insult before hitting the road.

Clarion's coach in the mid-1980s was Bob Bubb, who by the time of his team's whitewash over Edinboro already had achieved near-legendary status in college wrestling. Bubb's teams had finished among the top ten at the NCAA Division I tournament twice and he had coached three national champions. He would be named NCAA Division I national coach of the year in 1986, and nineteen years later following his retirement, he would be elected into the National Wrestling Hall of Fame. What's more, Bubb was part of the fabric of Pennsylvania's proud wrestling history. A native of Lock Haven, in the central Pennsylvania mountains that have long been the cradle of the sport in the state, Bubb was a state high school runner-up and later became an All-American at the University of Pittsburgh. He commanded respect everywhere he went, but especially back home, where his name was spoken with reverence, and still is.

Bubb rarely miscalculated, but he might have done so on this fateful night. After his Golden Eagles demolished an undermanned Edinboro team, Bubb sought permission to use the Scots' wrestling room, located in the basement of McComb Fieldhouse, the hulking, red-brick structure where Clarion had just embarrassed the hosts on a mat stretched across a wooden basketball floor. Down in the basement, in a padded room sticky from sweat and moist, heavy air, Bubb put his wrestlers through a practice. The implication was that the Golden Eagles hadn't been challenged by what had just happened upstairs. His message, intended or not, was received loud and clear by at least one senior member of Edinboro's administration, Athletic Director Jim McDonald, who began to stew almost immediately.

Bob Bubb knew college wrestling as well as anyone in the land, but he could not possibly have predicted where his decision to hold a post-match workout on that night in Edinboro might lead.

⊕ ⊕ ⊕ ⊕ ⊕

JIM MCDONALD WAS BORN IN BRIDGEPORT, WEST VIRGINIA, AND raised in the culture of basketball. By the time he graduated from high school, he was considered one of the best young players in the country, joining future NBA star Jerry West among the top college prospects in West Virginia. The long, lean McDonald became an All-American at West Virginia Wesleyan, finishing second in the nation in scoring, and was a late-round pick in the NBA draft. But instead of extending his playing career, McDonald decided to teach the game. He arrived at Edinboro in 1962 as the men's basketball coach and in twelve years never had a losing season. He became athletic director in 1981. It's fair to say that even after three years heading up an athletic program with a longstanding wrestling team, McDonald hadn't the slightest clue about either the sport itself or how its athletes trained at the highest levels. To McDonald, Edinboro's wrestling team was something largely foreign and misunderstood, a program run by Caro that basically cost very little money to operate and which almost entirely took care of itself, celebrating its wins and lamenting its losses mostly in obscurity.

That changed after the Clarion match.

McDonald might not have known wrestling, but he knew sports. He might not have understood what it meant to shoot a double-leg takedown on an opponent from the neutral position, but he knew how it felt to have his ego bruised, and make no mistake, Jim McDonald's ego was badly injured on the morning after the Golden Eagles hung a 57–0 loss on one of his school's sports teams, even if he didn't have the slightest idea how to tally up the score. By the mid-1980s, Edinboro's sixteen athletic programs were no strangers to winning. The football team was one of the most consistent in the PSAC's Western Division. The men's basketball program had won a string of division titles under McDonald, and the school's cross country programs were among Division II's elite. The school had a proud history of athletic success, and McDonald, fiercely proud himself, liked to advertise it. The walls in the main corridor of McComb Fieldhouse were plastered with framed photos and All-America certificates of the school's biggest stars. In the main gym, banners commemorating the school's conference championships and NCAA finishes hung from the rafters like wide, red icicles. To McDonald, a humiliating loss, even one absorbed by a secondary program like wrestling, carried a humbling sting, especially when it came at the hands of the Scots' closest conference rival. And especially when it was followed by what McDonald considered to be the ultimate slap in

Jim McDonald

the face—an opposing coach putting his team through its paces in one of Edinboro's athletic facilities because, ostensibly, the Scots hadn't put up enough of a fight.

McDonald had already been seething on the morning after the Clarion match when an athletic department aide brought him a clipping from that morning's *Pittsburgh Press,* one of two metropolitan newspapers in the closest large city to Edinboro. The *Press* routinely carried reports of PSAC wrestling matches, and while this story was modest, the headline was jarring. Above an account of the drubbing, the bold type shouted: "Clarion routs Edinboro, then practices."

McDonald was furious. He barely knew his way around small-time college wrestling, much less the logistics of competing in the sport at the Division I level, but he made up his mind, almost on the spot, that Edinboro was going to make a move. He was not sure how he could pay for it. He was not sure what sort of pitch he would have to make to Edinboro's upper administrators, whose budgets, like McDonald's, were chronically pinched by state funding allocations. He was not even sure how to talk to wrestling people. But he knew that if he had anything to say about it, Edinboro was not going to be on the wrong end of another 57–0 loss to a rival school. And he was not going to sit in his office and read a headline like the one he read that morning.

Still fuming, McDonald pulled out his NCAA directory and flipped through the pages. He wanted to talk to someone who could advise him on how Edinboro could make a push to become an elite wrestling school. He wanted someone to recommend a coach, to share some insight into what it would take to get a Division I program up and running. McDonald stopped flipping pages when he reached the section listing contact information for the University of Iowa. He slid his finger down the page and stopped, holding it next to the one name he knew from the world of big-time college wrestling: Dan Gable. Then he picked up the phone.

✣ ✣ ✣ ✣ ✣

On the floor of the Palace of Auburn Hills in March 2007, Gregor Gillespie was living out Jim McDonald's dream. A sophomore from outside Rochester, New York, Gillespie was overlooked by most of the major wrestling programs coming out of high school. Edinboro's coaches, who had made a nice living out of scouring for slightly raw but remarkable talents who slipped through the cracks in the blue-chip recruiting process, spotted something in Gillespie. More correctly, they sensed something in his makeup. Almost all Division I wrestlers are physical specimens, capable of training through exhaustion while simultaneously dieting to maintain their competitive weights. But what separates the average wrestler from the great one is a desire to win that cannot be coached or easily developed. It almost has to be innate, a competitive streak that drives him to believe he will not be beaten no matter how good the opponent is, no matter how high the stakes.

Edinboro's coaches recognized these qualities in Gillespie on their recruiting visits, and he rewarded them with a seventh-place finish at the 2006 national tournament, earning All-America honors as a true freshman. Such an accomplishment is rare at Edinboro, where the coaches are accustomed to getting wrestlers who need at least a red-shirt season to build up their strength, hone their skills, or bring their grades into NCAA compliance. Some do not blossom for two or three years, if at all. Gillespie, though, was one of those rare, nearly finished products, ready to win at the college level right out of high school. Edinboro had never had a true freshman like him.

He began his first college season with twenty-three straight victories before losing in the semifinals at the Southern Scuffle, an early season tournament in Greensboro, North Carolina. Gillespie lost another match at the Scuffle and finished a disappointing fifth, but there would be few other disappointments for him that season. His seventh-place finish made him the first true freshman ever to place at the nationals for the Scots, and he entered his sophomore season as a solid contender to crack the top six at his weight class. Still, going into the nationals at the Palace, even the most daring observers didn't have Gillespie favored to win. That was because of Minnesota's Schlatter, the sophomore phenom who emerged from the same national recruiting class as Gillespie but reached the top of the heap immediately, winning a national championship as a freshman. By the time he matched up with Gillespie in the 149-pound national semifinals, Schlatter had run off sixty-five straight wins dating to the first half of his freshman season, many of them lopsided. Schlatter looked simply unbeatable in the tournament, at least until he took the mat against Gillespie.

What Schlatter didn't know, though, was that Edinboro's coaches had been preparing Gillespie for the match for nine months. Starting early the previous summer, Head Coach Tim Flynn would make almost daily calls to Gillespie's cell phone pretending to be Schlatter.

"Hi, this is Dustin Schlatter," Flynn would say into the phone. "I'm just wondering—should I even bother showing up in Detroit next March, or can I just have them mail the medal to me?"

Gregor Gillespie waits for the winning takedown call in overtime of the 2007 NCAA 149-pound final against Michigan's Josh Churella. (Courtesy Edinboro University)

It was silly, and Flynn knew it. Gillespie, too.

But Flynn kept it up because he wanted the silliness of the calls to turn into irritation for Gillespie. And he wanted that irritation to turn into a burning desire to beat Schlatter, a star from one of college wrestling's privileged programs. Teams like Minnesota were accustomed to sending their wrestlers onto the mat against opponents from small schools like Edinboro, methodically dismantling them, and moving on. Minnesota, like other top Big Ten and Big 12 programs, brings in some of the best recruits in the country every year. Schools like Edinboro are left to fight over the kids who do not get major-college offers. They might turn out a great wrestler every few years, but logic would suggest that Edinboro's best should not be able to beat Minnesota's best, and clearly that's what Schlatter was.

But that didn't stop Flynn's head games. Silly as they were,

Flynn's calls to Gillespie were calculated. He wanted Gillespie to not only want to beat Schlatter, but also to feel he had to beat him—not just to prove to himself he could win, but also to get his coaches off of his back.

"I knew why he was calling me," Gillespie said of Flynn. "I understood what he was trying to do. But it was still annoying. After a while, you just want to shut somebody up."

In the national semifinals, in an enormous arena in Michigan on a cold Friday night in March 2007, Gillespie's chance to silence his coach had finally arrived.

Jim McDonald could not have fathomed it at the time. But this was precisely the moment he had envisioned twenty-three years earlier, when he made a bold move inspired by a stinging loss and Bob Bubb's rare moment of indiscretion.

| Chapter Two |

"Iowa of the East"

I F A BASKETBALL GUY LIKE JIM MCDONALD WAS ONLY GOING TO know one name from big-time college wrestling in the mid-1980s, Dan Gable was a good name to know. Even some thirty-five years after Gable won a gold medal at the 1972 Olympic Games in Munich without surrendering a single point in the tournament, Gable's name remained the standard by which all other wrestlers—Bruce Baumgartner, John Smith, and Cael Sanderson included—are measured. Walk into any high school wrestling room in the country and you would be hard pressed to find someone who hasn't heard Gable's legendary story, in much the same way that a student studying early American history surely would encounter the tale of George Washington crossing the Delaware. Only in Gable's case, everything is carefully, sometimes painfully, documented, from his devastating loss in the NCAA final his senior year—the first and only defeat of his college career—to his Lazarus-like rise at the international level that produced perhaps the most dominant performance in the history of the Games, his gold medal-winning run at the 1972 Munich Olympics.

In wrestling he was known simply as "Gable," and if you had happened to train under him at Iowa, you were known as one of Gable's men, a title that came with no small amount of respect. Any wrestler trained in Gable's Iowa program could be counted on to be tough, resilient, relentless, and fearless. Any wrestler whose career Gable touched would carry that with him forever, and it was sometimes enough to provide a psychological edge over an opponent before either wrestler stepped onto the mat. At the time McDonald decided his Edinboro wrestling program needed

Undated photo of coach Mike DeAnna (R) with one of his first blue-chip
recruits, Terry Kennedy (L), before a home match. Assistant coach Bruce
Baumgartner is in the background.

an upgrade, Baumgartner was still months from winning his first
Olympic gold, Smith was an eighteen-year-old high school senior
in Del City, Oklahoma, and Sanderson was a five year old making
the rounds at youth tournaments in Utah. If there was someone
to turn to for advice on how to build greatness in college wrestling
it was Gable, and while McDonald didn't know him personally, he
knew him by reputation, and that was enough.

McDonald later admitted he was somewhat stunned to get
Gable on the phone on his first try on that bitter cold morning
in the winter of 1984, the morning after Edinboro had been
trounced at home, 57–0, by one of its closest conference rivals.
Gable's Iowa team was in the middle of its season, in the middle
of a run of dominance that saw the Hawkeyes win nine straight
national championships, and McDonald knew the man at the

helm of college wrestling's most successful program would be busy no matter the time of day. But Gable answered, and McDonald, after identifying himself, launched into a pitch he had little time to rehearse.

"I want to start a Division I wrestling program," McDonald began. "I'm calling you because my school is about to drop wrestling, and I want to go in the other direction and start a big-time program. I want to find the best wrestling coach in the United States. I want to build the best wrestling program in the Eastern United States. I want to compete with Iowa. I want to be the Iowa of the East."

There was a long, uncomfortable silence on Gable's end of the line.

"How much are you willing to spend?" Gable finally responded.

"Whatever it takes."

Gable was silent again. McDonald thought he heard him chuckle. He needed to convince Gable this was no joke.

"You have a wrestling office?" Gable asked.

"We'll build one."

"You have a weight room?"

"We'll put one in."

"You have locker rooms?"

"We'll get them."

"You have a recruiting budget?"

"We'll create one."

Silence.

McDonald would have to forgive Gable's skepticism.

In 1984, college wrestling was reeling. Gable knew programs were being cut at an alarming rate. By the mid-1990s, three hundred schools dropped the sport either to save money or to comply with Title IX gender equity issues—or both. Gable knew that even at the top of the college wrestling world, some of the better programs were learning to get by with less, yet here was an athletic director from a tiny Division II school in Pennsylvania insisting he was prepared to dump as much money as he needed into building a program from scratch.

After a few minutes, Gable realized this was no joke. McDonald was serious about piecing together a wrestling powerhouse that could eventually compete with Iowa, and he was bold enough to ask the Hawkeyes' coach for the blueprint. Near the end of their conversation, after McDonald had quizzed Gable some more about what he would need to get a Division I program off the ground—all things Edinboro didn't have; all things McDonald still wasn't sure how or if he could pay for—the Edinboro athletic director had one more question: Whom would Gable recommend to run the thing?

"The best young wrestling coach in the country is on my staff," Gable replied. "His name is Mike DeAnna."

DeAnna's credentials were impeccable. He grew up in Bay Village, Ohio, a Cleveland suburb in the middle of one of high school wrestling's hotbeds. In terms of the sheer number of talented wrestlers and coaches produced each year, you could do no better than Pennsylvania and Ohio, neighboring states who engaged in a constant game of comparisons to declare which was the country's most fertile ground for top-notch college talent. DeAnna grew up in that culture. His father, Lino, had been an Ohio high school state champion in 1953 and had passed along his love of the sport to his son when Mike turned nine years old. A natural athlete who played just about anything that was in season, Mike DeAnna quickly latched on to wrestling because it satisfied something inside him he could never find in team competition. As far back as he could remember, DeAnna had been fascinated by the intense, individual battles in sports—the mano-a-mano of pitcher-batter duels in baseball, the violent baseline volleys in tennis, and, of course, the intimate, grueling hand-to-hand combat in wrestling.

"People ask me all the time what my favorite things are," DeAnna said years after leaving Edinboro. "I tell them besides being with my family, it's listening to baseball on the radio, sitting courtside at a tennis match, and being out on the mat."

DeAnna's competitive juices could really flow in wrestling, and by the time his high school career came to a close, he was a three-time Ohio state champion good enough to be recruited by

Dan Gable's Hawkeye wrestling machine. Iowa and DeAnna were a good fit. He was ready for the physical abuse that comes with training at the Division I level and the overwhelming challenge of proving himself in the toughest wrestling practice room in the country. And Gable was the man who could make him the best at his weight class. That DeAnna never won an NCAA title at Iowa was almost immaterial. He had bought completely into the simple yet brutally effective Iowa philosophy of hard work in the practice room and relentlessness on the mat. By his early twenties, when his college career had wound down and he had begun to train and compete internationally in pursuit of a spot on the U.S. Olympic freestyle team, DeAnna already had started to hone his coaching skills as recruiting coordinator on Iowa's staff. Gable recognized these coaching skills in DeAnna and knew that he was a born promoter. Gable saw in his former wrestler the traits McDonald would need from a coach trying to launch a Division I wrestling program basically from scratch.

The timing was such that when McDonald called Gable, Iowa was preparing to head east to New Jersey, site of the NCAA tournament. DeAnna and his wife, Pam, a former Hawkeye Mat Maid born and bred in Iowa, left their two children with a babysitter and drove to the nationals. They stopped in Edinboro on their way. The two knew nothing about the tiny town. They knew nothing about the little Division II school with the athletic director who dreamed of butting heads with college wrestling's most established and most successful powers. They knew nothing about Jim McDonald, but they were about to find out.

✢ ✢ ✢ ✢ ✢

DEANNA AGREED TO INTERVIEW FOR THE EDINBORO JOB ALMOST solely on Gable's recommendation. It wasn't easy, after all, to ignore advice from the most visible man in the wrestling world, especially since before even visiting the campus DeAnna recognized the opportunity to be closer to home and to put his stamp on a program that might be built in Iowa's image. Not only that, but there was no guarantee that DeAnna would have a job after that year's Olympic

Trials, and he had a wife and two kids to take care of. So on a March morning in 1984, Mike DeAnna steered his brown Buick Century station wagon off Interstate 79, the main artery between Pittsburgh and Erie, wound down a long hill on a two-lane road past the town's only hotel—a Holiday Inn—past two golf courses and a small plaza, past the headwaters of Edinboro Lake, a glacial lake encircled by tiny cottages, a few beaches, and some makeshift marinas. He and Pam drove through one of the two stoplights in town, past the historic Crossroads Dinor, the McDonald's restaurant and the Copper Coin bar. About half a mile east of the town's center, they turned onto a sprawling, picturesque campus whose most distinguishing features were Sox Harrison Stadium— home to the university's successful Division II football team—and twin ten-story dormitories known as Lawrence Towers. McComb Fieldhouse was near the geographic center of campus, adjacent to an oversized, man-made pond. The DeAnnas parked and walked inside, prepared to listen to Jim McDonald try to sell Mike on the wisdom of leaving the center of the college wrestling universe, a place where elite, world-class training partners were minutes away; of uprooting his wife from her home state; and of taking over a program at a school that had never been remotely exposed to the level of training and competition DeAnna and Gable had come to expect.

Inside a conference room on the main floor of McComb Fieldhouse, just around the corner from the gymnasium where, several weeks earlier, Clarion had rocked Edinboro's world and launched McDonald into an angry, embarrassment-fueled search for atonement, the athletic director and former basketball coach was waiting with a group of school officials that included David O'Dessa, the school's vice president of administration, a charter member of the school's athletic hall of fame who had the ear of Edinboro's president, Foster Diebold. After introductions were made and some polite small talk was out of the way, McDonald cut to the chase, following roughly the line of questioning he had put to Gable on the phone.

When DeAnna asked about salary, McDonald told him whatever he was making at the time, whatever other offers he had,

Edinboro would beat them.

Assistant coaches?

Hire the best you can find, McDonald said. We'll pay them accordingly.

Travel?

McDonald pledged to let the new coach take his team across the country, if need be, to find top recruits and the best competition.

Scholarships?

The program would be fully funded, McDonald said.

Facilities? DeAnna had just finished a walking tour of the campus and of McComb Fieldhouse. He saw the wresting operation, which was Spartan, at best. He didn't notice a weight room.

"Everything you need will be here," McDonald promised. "I'll make it happen."

At that point, about an hour into the interview, McDonald was feeling his oats. He had gone to Diebold and won Diebold's blessing to upgrade the program. He had O'Dessa's support. He had, across a shiny oak table, the man he believed possessed the pedigree and the passion to turn his dream of fielding a top-notch Division I wrestling program into reality. All he needed was a commitment, and Jim McDonald wasn't shy about asking for one. Or expecting it on the spot.

None was forthcoming. DeAnna was impressed but unsure. And he wouldn't budge.

"The interview couldn't have gone much worse," DeAnna recalled years later. "He wanted an answer yesterday, and I wasn't prepared to give him one."

The pivotal moment came when McDonald, convinced DeAnna was his man, asked if there was anything else he would need to win.

Anything more he needed to know?

No, DeAnna said. Nothing.

McDonald offered the job.

The response? Nothing.

DeAnna looked at his wife, looked around, and thought of all the people he wanted to consult. He mentioned to McDonald that he

wanted to talk to his friends and former teammates back in Iowa—
Joe Gonzales, John Azevedo—some of the most accomplished
wrestlers and coaches in the world, men whose judgment he trusted,
to ask their opinions and gauge their interest in potentially coming
along to assist him. He wanted to talk to Gable.

Hearing what he assumed to be a stall tactic, McDonald rose
from his chair. His face reddened. His patience was stretched.

"I don't know who this Jose Gonzales fellow is," McDonald
roared in a moment of legendary political incorrectness. "All I
know is that you've been sucking from Dan Gable's milk bottle all
your life. You need to grow up and become a man!"

McDonald was rolling the dice by questioning the manhood
of an elite athlete, an Olympic-caliber wrestler with a sparkling
resume in a sport in which questioning one's manhood didn't
always go over so well. But McDonald pressed on. He knew Mike
and Pam DeAnna still had to drive across Pennsylvania and into
New Jersey and would have plenty of time to talk themselves out
of coming to Edinboro. He knew once they got back home to
Iowa City where Pam's family lived, it would be easier to say no,
after the hours and the miles had worn the initial charm off the
ego-stroking thrill of starting a Division I program from next to
nothing. McDonald knew he was taking a chance, but he stayed
on DeAnna nonetheless.

"They've got phones all along the turnpike," McDonald
said brusquely and with the self-assuredness of a man who knew
exactly what he was doing. "You've got four hours. If I don't hear
from you, I'm going to the next best assistant coach in the country
and I'm going to hire him. And if he doesn't take it, I'll go to the
next-best guy and I'll hire him. I'm going to find a guy who is
willing to take on this challenge. This is a great opportunity. You've
basically got free reign to do whatever you need to do to build this
program, as long you don't break the rules. If you don't want it, I'll
find someone who does."

Mike DeAnna was stunned. Pam didn't know what to say. The
two walked out of McComb Fieldhouse without giving McDonald
an answer.

"We walked out the door and my wife looked at me and said,

'You were terrible,'" DeAnna recalled.

Pam knew Mike hadn't hit it off with McDonald and was afraid he had angered him by refusing to accept the job on the spot.

The two got in their car and headed out of Edinboro. They didn't know if they would ever return. Mike was concerned about making a misstep, about leaving the security blanket of Iowa's program and the steady, if unrelenting, presence that Gable represented. He was worried about the Olympics, which were coming up that summer, and how we would continue his training. He was worried about Pam, who was convinced her husband had just crashed and burned in his first opportunity at a Division I coaching job, a goal he had pointed toward for as long as she had known him. The two talked. It was bittersweet. At one point, Pam DeAnna looked out the car window at the rolling Pennsylvania countryside dotted with trees and dairy farms. She was feeling very, very far from home.

"There are no cornfields here," she said to Mike.

Then, she began to cry.

|Chapter Three|

First Steps

U<small>NDER</small> DIFFERENT CIRCUMSTANCES, M<small>IKE</small> D<small>E</small>A<small>NNA</small> WOULD
have returned to Iowa after the nationals and spent a few fitful
days thinking about whether to accept Jim McDonald's challenge
to build Edinboro's fledgling Division I wrestling program into
a national power. DeAnna would have talked to close friends
like Joe Gonzales and John Azevedo and asked them whether
the opportunity to put his stamp on an upstart team at a small
Pennsylvania school outweighed the risk of attaching his name
and his Iowa stock to a test vehicle that, for all DeAnna knew, was
just as likely to veer off the road into an ugly pileup as succeed,
potentially scaring off coaches and athletic directors who might
be wary of hiring someone who couldn't get the job done the first
time. At the very least, DeAnna would have taken a few days to
make calls to potential assistant coaches, to test the waters and find
out who among his friends and contemporaries might be willing to
take the plunge at his side.

But McDonald wasn't giving him that luxury. McDonald was
giving him four hours.

When DeAnna drove away from McComb Fieldhouse that
afternoon in March 1984, he was on the clock. McDonald had
dangled in front of the twenty-six-year-old DeAnna—the former
high school and college wrestling champion—a tantalizing carrot
that he threatened to take away if DeAnna didn't meet his deadline.
And so, with a tearful Pam in the passenger's seat and miles of
road stretching through the Pennsylvania countryside in front of
him, DeAnna wrestled with the decision of whether to leave the
security blanket that Iowa and Gable provided for what might be

Bruce Baumgartner and Edinboro athletic director Jim McDonald at
McComb Fieldhouse in 1992.

a once-in-a-lifetime opportunity to make a name for himself at a
school that was adding Division I wrestling when so many others
were taking it away.

He and Pam talked some more and decided they had to do
what was best for their young family, which faced an uncertain
future after that summer's Olympics. If it meant Pam had to leave
her family, her beloved Iowa, for a place some fourteen hours away,
she was willing to do so to help spark Mike's coaching career.

Convinced he could not afford to pass up an opportunity, and
creeping up on McDonald's time limit, DeAnna pulled the Buick
off the turnpike and parked at a rest stop.

He found a pay phone.

And then he made the call.

Back in Edinboro, on the other end of the line, McDonald

was delighted. He had, in his mind, just landed the best young college coaching prospect in the country, a kid stamped with the endorsement of a legend in the sport. DeAnna had spent nearly a third of his life in Iowa's wrestling room soaking up wisdom and punishment, all the while imagining how he might someday put what he had learned to use building his own program—which tortuous drills to put his wrestlers through and which choice words to say after a long, brutal training session to build back up his athletes before they trudged off to their dorms, hungry and exhausted, to make them want to come back the next day for more of the same.

DeAnna had made it clear to McDonald and the other members of Edinboro's search committee that he believed he was ready to create a winner, that he had a plan to get the Scots up and running quickly, both on and off the mat. DeAnna wasn't interested in a slow, steady ascent. While he understood that sustaining success at Edinboro would take time and careful block-building through recruiting and fund-raising, he also understood the college wrestling landscape well enough to know that it was possible to make a splash—and to win—right away. He knew there were wrestlers tucked away at places like Iowa and Oklahoma State who had never gotten the opportunity to compete because in some cases the wrestler in front of them was only minimally better. He knew that in some cases they were stuck behind national champions or title contenders who had edged them in wrestle-offs, relegating them to the obscurity of backup status, of wrestling in open tournaments and serving as training partners until the starter was injured or used up his eligibility. DeAnna knew some of those men personally. He knew that, given the chance, they could make their own names and compete for their own championships at a place like Edinboro, a place with few guarantees but plenty of opportunities.

DeAnna already was targeting Hawkeyes like Mike Hahesy, a backup who won an Iowa schoolboy title but lost a series of close wrestle-offs, keeping him out of the Hawkeyes' lineup. Hahesy might well have been one of the three or four best 157-pounders in the country, but few outside of Iowa City knew it because he had always competed in the shadows. These were the wrestlers—hungry, talented, in need of a break—that DeAnna knew he needed to bring in to make Edinboro competitive right away. He would sprinkle them in among promising recruits who would see their training habits and recognize their relentless drive to compete and win. On that foundation, DeAnna believed he could build a program that eventually would sustain itself, one that after four or five years would find and develop its own talented wrestlers and take them to the nationals and watch them climb high on the medal stand. DeAnna was convinced he could do it, and the challenge appealed to the same part of him that drove him in the training room and on the mat. DeAnna knew some people would condemn him and Edinboro to failure before their first official competition, just as some might have dismissed his chances before he won his first Ohio state title or earned his first All-America certificate at Iowa. His juices flowed when he thought about proving them wrong.

But before any of this could happen—the recruiting, the transfers, the I-told-you-sos—DeAnna needed to find an assistant coach.

⊕   ⊕   ⊕   ⊕   ⊕

In sizing up DeAnna, Jim McDonald relied heavily on two things: Dan Gable's endorsement and his own gut. McDonald, the former basketball coach, knew enough about Gable to believe that if DeAnna carried a recommendation from the legendary coach, he would know everything a coach would need to know to teach Edinboro's wrestlers how to win. But at any Division I wrestling school, there was considerably more to the job—and doubly so at Edinboro. Unlike football and basketball, Division I wrestling was not a revenue sport. Unlike football, it did not generate enough money to allow the largest schools to offset their entire athletic budgets through five or six home football games along with a hefty bowl check and perhaps some local or national television revenue. Unlike basketball, it did not attract the networks and ESPN to campus with their cameras and their well-groomed reporters and commentators in tow to expose a school's athletes to an audience of millions, capping the season with a nationally televised championship tournament steeped in history that stretched on for weeks and, for the best teams, provided the kind of exposure the best marketing campaign could never hope to match. To the contrary, wrestling was a financial loss leader. Even the greatest college wrestling powers cost much more than they brought in, existing to help round out the athletic offerings at their schools or to maintain hard-won national reputations. The biggest schools in the Big Ten and Big 8 sunk hundreds of thousands of dollars into recruiting budgets and coaches' salaries and facilities upgrades, and most of the money came from their football receipts or from private endowments secured by wrestling coaches and alumni through fund raisers and gifts. Although this would change years later, the NCAA tournament was, in the mid-1980s, little more than a curiosity on college sports' main stage. Few outside of wrestling's inner circle of fans cared to watch. Fewer still appreciated what they saw.

For those reasons, McDonald understood long before he met DeAnna that the man who ultimately would head up his school's newborn Division I program would have to be part wrestling coach, part promoter. He would need to have a publicist's tact, a Madison Avenue sales executive's brain, and a circus purveyor's knack for getting a skeptical audience to watch his show. McDonald had done the homework on his end, convincing university president Foster Diebold to pledge $100,000 to fund the wrestling program's operating budget that first year—including $40,000 in scholarships—and to sink thousands more into facilities to upgrade the shoestring operation the school had allowed it to become. He had sold Diebold and his right-hand man, vice president David O'Dessa, on the need to build a weight room and a coaching suite, two things Gable and DeAnna insisted were vital to attract and keep good recruits and top-flight young coaches. Diebold had gone along with McDonald's plan, with the understanding that the new coach and his staff would go into the community and convince existing Edinboro athletic boosters to invest in the new program, to find new blood to pump money into McDonald's vision. "He wanted results," DeAnna recalled of McDonald. "And I wanted to win. It was a good combination."

The new coach also would face some uneasiness on a campus that did not have a Division I athletic program and might not know how to react to one. Edinboro's track, cross country, football, and basketball programs all had achieved success at one time or another, but never under the kind of spotlight that Division I wrestling could bring—and not at that cost. The Pennsylvania State Athletic Conference (PSAC) was a strong Division II conference, but aside from wrestling it was also very provincial. PSAC teams seldom traveled beyond the five-state area that included Pennsylvania, New York, Ohio, West Virginia, and Maryland for regular-season games. Plane trips were relatively unheard of. Yet competing at the highest levels of college wrestling would mean traveling to places like Las Vegas and Florida, the Midwest, and wherever that year's NCAA tournament happened to be held. While Edinboro maintained its wrestling ties to the PSAC, the program joined the Eastern Wrestling League in 1989, putting it in the company of major schools like West Virginia and Pittsburgh and further upping the ante. Recruits would need to be unearthed, evaluated, and courted potentially anywhere in the country. In order to compete with the massive, well-funded programs from the Big Ten and Big 12, Edinboro would have to pamper its wrestlers to some degree, and that would take money. McDonald and DeAnna, even before they met, understood that for a school like Edinboro the investment came with a payoff that could be immense. While wrestling probably would never be a revenue sport, its ability to thrust the tiny campus and its relatively obscure programs to a national and even an international stage would be priceless. Within just a few years after McDonald elevated the program, Edinboro would host all-star matches pitting some of the world's best Olympic freestyle wrestlers against the best from the United States. Even the legendary Gable and his Hawkeyes—the greatest road show in college wrestling—would visit McComb Fieldhouse for a dual meet against the Scots. This was heady, high-profile stuff, and there was sure to be both curiosity and resentment from within the athletic department and the campus at large.

So the new coach would need to be thick-skinned, too. McDonald knew this. Soon enough, DeAnna would know it, too.

☥   ☥   ☥   ☥   ☥

As much as Dan Gable hated to see Mike DeAnna leave Iowa, he knew it was the right move for his former wrestler. DeAnna was a young man on a staff loaded with talented young men, and at the time Gable was nowhere near ready to step down. The chances for advancement at Iowa for DeAnna were slim, and Gable recognized in DeAnna an aptitude he might not fully develop if he stayed with the Hawkeyes. So when DeAnna rejoined Gable at the nationals in New Jersey and told the legendary coach that he had decided to take the Edinboro job, Gable was both happy for DeAnna and sad to let him go.

"He was one of my best," Gable later recalled. "He was one of those kids who you knew would be great for the sport. His [competitive] career was [nearly] over, but he had much, much more to give. It was the right decision."

Pam DeAnna, born and raised amid Iowa cornfields and a Hawkeye in her heart and soul, had a little more trouble making the move. Although her husband was from Cleveland, only a two-hour drive from Edinboro, she was leaving home to go to a place where she knew no one and where no one knew her. Still, like Gable, she understood this was an opportunity Mike could not afford to pass up. In Edinboro, he had a chance to build a program at a time when so many around the country were being dismantled, a chance to take what he learned under Gable and apply it in his own way, to his own wrestlers, in his own practice room. As she had in Iowa, where she was a Mat Maid, she threw herself fully behind her husband's new program.

Meanwhile, Mike DeAnna had already moved well past the decision to take the job and was thinking about what he needed to do. He faced an awesome challenge. First, he needed an assistant coach, someone who could both help him sell the program around the country and help him train and develop Edinboro's wrestlers once they got them in their room. He needed someone to bond quickly with the locals and help them feel ownership of the program, and he needed someone he could trust, since so much would be at stake in the early weeks and months. At the time, DeAnna was also training for the Olympic Trials and what he hoped would be a spot on the U.S. freestyle team at the 1984 Summer Olympics in Los Angeles. He would be pushing himself to exhaustion two or three times a day in his workouts, and in between trying to lay the groundwork for the program that would be awaiting his arrival in August, when the Olympics ended.

DeAnna and McDonald agreed that DeAnna would remain in Iowa City to train and conduct business from there. In Iowa, he would be better suited to scout for an assistant coach, and he would be closer to the network of contacts that could help him land potential transfers and recruits that would help Edinboro compete right away. McDonald gave him a phone card and a mandate—find talent and bring it to Pennsylvania in the fall. DeAnna arrived back in Iowa with little time to catch his breath. He had a short list of potential assistant coaches, and it included his friends Joe Gonzales and John Azevedo, two lighter weight wrestlers who, in DeAnna's mind, would complement DeAnna's ability to work with Edinboro's middle- and upper-weights.

DeAnna knew it would be a tough sell. Most young coaches were looking to catch on as a volunteer or second assistant with a Big Ten or Big 12 program with a clear path to moving up the ladder. Going to a place as obscure as Edinboro, even as the No. 2 man, wasn't particularly inviting. Ever the pitchman, DeAnna worked his friends and contemporaries, trying to sell them on becoming a part of something fresh and new. No one took the bait. Gonzalez and Azevedo both were former NCAA champions and had the qualifications DeAnna was seeking. But both were Californians, and neither expressed to DeAnna much interest in trekking east of the Mississippi River to join a program that, at the time, seemed to be surrounded by more questions than answers.

Finally, DeAnna found someone who would listen, a mountain of a young man from New Jersey, by way of Indiana State, a man who, like DeAnna, was training for the Olympics and working as an assistant in one of college wrestling's privileged programs.

✠ ✠ ✠ ✠ ✠

A LATE BLOOMER AND RELATIVE LATECOMER TO WRESTLING, Bruce Baumgartner took up the sport in ninth grade, joining the varsity team at Manchester Regional High School in his hometown of Haledon, N.J. At 190 pounds as a high school freshman, Baumgartner had been too big to play peewee football and not terribly interested in baseball, and he turned to wrestling, essentially, because his other sporting options weren't all that attractive.

His father, Robert Sr., was a diesel mechanic, and sports were never pushed hard on Baumgartner and his brother Bob growing up. But in wrestling he found a niche, a sport where his size helped more than it held him back, and he blossomed on the mats. Baumgartner never won a state championship in high school, but the combination of size and athleticism and his willingness to train allowed him to rise to a third-place finish in the state as a senior, a remarkable accomplishment for someone who had only spent four years in a sport that many children take up in grade school. Baumgartner caught the eye of recruiters, and he accepted a scholarship offer from Indiana State, the school Larry Bird had helped put on the map as a Division I basketball star in the early 1980s.

Baumgartner learned how to fully capitalize on his combination of strength and balance at Indiana State. He was a heavyweight, but he didn't move like one. His ability to score and scramble out of tough holds made him a handful for slower, lumbering opponents. Yet his size—around 260 pounds by the end of his college career—was more than most of them could handle. He turned himself into an NCAA champion by his senior year, beating Oklahoma's Steve Williams 4–2 in the national finals to cap a 44–0 season in 1982. An industrial arts major, Baumgartner was handy, a craftsman who probably could have done well for himself working in the building trades or as a high school wood shop teacher. But wrestling had taken hold of him, and he knew after graduating that he was not finished with the sport.

Instead, Baumgartner joined the coaching staff at Oklahoma State University, becoming a graduate assistant at one of wrestling's top programs. At Oklahoma State, Baumgartner had access to world-class facilities and world-class training partners as he prepared for his next goal—making the U.S. freestyle team and competing in the 1984 Summer Games in Los Angeles.

With his wife, Linda, a graduate assistant athletic trainer at Oklahoma State, Baumgartner was content to stay in Stillwater for the time being and train for international competition while learning the subtleties of teaching and coaching the sport under OSU Coach Tommy Chesbro, who had led the Cowboys to eight Big Eight titles and a national championship in fifteen seasons. OSU was steeped in tradition, the only program in the country with more national titles than Iowa, the only program in college wrestling whose profile rose to meet the Hawkeyes. Baumgartner, who was quickly becoming a student of the sport, could appreciate everything Stillwater had to offer.

Then Chesbro was unexpectedly let go, and OSU hired Joe Seay, who offered Baumgartner the chance to stay on as a fourth or fifth assistant coach. To Baumgartner, it amounted to a demotion, and it left him with limited options.

In the big picture, Baumgartner hoped to train and coach for several more years before retiring from the sport, at which time he expected to move back east, closer to his New Jersey roots, and settle down somewhere as a high school industrial arts teacher.

And then he met Mike DeAnna.

Baumgartner knew of DeAnna from wrestling circles. You could not compete at the sport at the elite level for as many years as DeAnna and Baumgartner had and not cross paths, hear of one another by reputation, meet, and exchange how-do-you-dos. But he really got to know him in the spring of 1984 at Iowa, where Baumgartner went to train in preparation for the upcoming World Cup.

Simply by being in Iowa's practice room every day, Baumgartner had overheard some of the buzz about Edinboro. He heard Gable talking about a small school out east that was trying to go big time, and he heard that DeAnna had signed on to be its coach. Baumgartner didn't think much of it until one day, when the two were chatting after a workout, DeAnna asked if he might be interested in joining him in Pennsylvania.

"Have them send me some information," Baumgartner told DeAnna. "I'll take a look."

Baumgartner was preparing to compete at the World Cup, one of the important pre-Olympic tournaments that sorted out the contenders for the U.S. national team.

The top-ranked U.S. heavyweight after earning four international silver or bronze medals in 1983 and capturing the 1984 AAU nationals, Baumgartner was a strong favorite to win, but where he might be headed after returning from the World Cup suddenly seemed far less certain.

| Chapter Four |

Baptisms

AFTER RETURNING FROM THE WORLD CUP, WHERE HE WON THE heavyweight title to establish himself as a favorite for Olympic gold, Baumgartner packed another suitcase and, along with Linda, headed east to Edinboro to talk to Jim McDonald about becoming Mike DeAnna's top assistant at the fledgling Division I program.

The Baumgartners were practical people, and they had their priorities. Aside from the job, Bruce and Linda wanted to be certain Edinboro was the sort of town where they could be comfortable. They had no intention of renting a small apartment someplace near the campus and blending in to the transient crowds that make up so much of the college population. They wanted to buy a house and establish roots, even if it was just for a few years, since they had no real idea how long they would be staying.

So in the middle of a particularly miserable stretch of cold, wet weather in April 1984, Bruce and Linda Baumgartner arrived in Edinboro, spent the night in a fixed-up room in Jim McDonald's basement, and set out with the athletic director to explore the campus and do some house-hunting the next day.

After touring the existing wrestling room and the makeshift office in the dungeon-like basement of McComb Fieldhouse, McDonald drove the Baumgartners through a rainstorm into the countryside a few miles outside of town. Along Kinter Hill Road, a two-lane highway stretching east of campus through rolling farmland, Bruce Baumgartner spotted the house he had seen in the real estate listings. The group pulled over, and Baumgartner slogged through ankle-deep mud to inspect the property. It was perfect, a fixer-upper that would allow him to do some woodworking and renovation, close to campus yet out of the way enough to provide a bit of a haven for a blossoming international star who was becoming a name but who still protected and treasured his privacy.

McDonald offered the job, and the somewhat shy, reserved Baumgartner was going to take it—the position, the house, and the challenge of joining DeAnna, the born promoter, in helping place Edinboro's wrestling program on the map. But not yet.

Instead, he told McDonald that he wanted to return to Oklahoma and think it over, take some time for him and Linda to absorb what the move would mean, both personally and professionally. They had a lot going on, and they were about to be homeless for a few months. They had checked out of married student housing at Oklahoma State, put their belongings in storage and left for a series of training stops leading up to the Olympic Games.

Certainly McDonald would understand their desire to think it over, Baumgartner thought.

Maybe they should have talked to the DeAnnas.

McDonald, not surprisingly, was getting itchy. He had in place his head coach, a man he believed to be the most qualified in the country, and he was ready to see the program move forward with its recruiting and make inroads into the Edinboro community. McDonald was not patient, and even though it would take a full two seasons for his wrestling program to make the jump from Division II to Division I status, he wanted his coaches to get to work right away.

"He was a pit bull," Baumgartner said. "He would call me almost every day and ask if I was going to take it. And then he would call back with another raise. I think he thought he was overpaying, but in the world of Division I athletics he wasn't really overpaying. The number one assistant at Oklahoma State was making significantly more than I signed for."

Yet Baumgartner took the job. He called the realtor and made an offer on the house on Kinter Hill Road, a place that he and Linda would spend the next twelve years restoring and remodeling, and he called Jim McDonald to say they had a deal.

Then he left for the Olympics.

Edinboro's coaching staff was in place. Now the real work was about to begin.

✢ ✢ ✢ ✢ ✢

DURING HIS PHONE CONVERSATION WITH DAN GABLE IN JANUARY 1984, Jim McDonald had accepted Gable's invitation to be his guest in Iowa for a week, to watch DeAnna train, to see firsthand and close-up what Division I wrestling was all about, to get a glimpse of the things that would be happening in the basement of McComb Fieldhouse later that year.

In early March of that year, a few weeks after he had hired DeAnna and a few weeks before he landed Baumgartner, McDonald took Gable up on his offer and caught a flight to Iowa City to watch the Hawkeyes make their final preparations for the nationals.

For McDonald, the plane might as well have landed on Mars. What he experienced over the next several days was unlike anything he had seen in a lifetime of playing and coaching sports.

These wrestlers were insane. They awoke before dawn for practice at Iowa's Carver Hawkeye Arena, ran themselves to the point of exhaustion, sometimes vomiting into garbage cans while Gable and his coaches prodded them to finish emptying their stomach contents and keep on pushing, all in an effort to trick their minds into believing they weren't as tired as their bodies told them they were.

After class, they were back in the practice room, endlessly drilling move after move in a steamy, enclosed chamber of horrors that left the wrestlers' shirts drenched with sweat and blood and turned their faces into shock absorbers. Some had scars above their eyes from poundings they had absorbed in training or competition. Many bore the wrestlers' badge of honor, grotesquely misshapen ear cartilage caused by repeated blows, a condition known as cauliflower ear for the puffy, permanent swelling it leaves behind.

McDonald had seen wrestling practices before, but he had seen nothing like this.

"He walked around kind of like a puppy dog," Gable said. "His eyes were big, and he didn't really talk to anybody. He stayed close to the wall and just kind of watched."

The Iowa wrestlers went at each other like lions, and Gable was their trainer. He was known for pushing his teams to overcome whatever doubts they might have about their ability to win, to erase their fears and channel their focus solely on one thing—not injuries, not fatigue, not the strength of the competition, but only on executing their moves and winning. There was no place in Division I wrestling for the weak-minded, and there was no place in Iowa's practice room for the weak-minded wrestler to hide. Fortune would find him. Pain, too.

McDonald had played alongside and coached gifted athletes at Edinboro and in West Virginia. He had seen some of the best talent Division II had to offer, but he had never seen anyone push themselves through the limits like these wrestlers did, and he was both excited and a little concerned about what it would be like to have them doing it at Edinboro that fall.

"I was amazed that their training was actually much more difficult than their competitions," McDonald recalled. "And their competitions were incredibly hard."

But the training was only part of it. McDonald had seen athletes work themselves to exhaustion before. But in few other sports—perhaps in no other sport—did they do so while counting every calorie they put into their bodies, while denying themselves the food and liquid they needed to fully recover from their tortuous workouts.

The unsightly truth in college wrestling is that many of the athletes find themselves caught in cycles of binging and starvation. Many compete in weight classes twenty or more pounds lighter than their normal weights. In the mid-1980s, before the NCAA tightened rules on weight loss, it was not uncommon to see a 167-pound wrestler balloon to 200 pounds during the offseason, only to have to cut that weight back off of his body in time for a doctor to certify him as fit to safely compete at his desired weight class that winter.

This is a particularly tough adjustment for young college

wrestlers, who are accustomed to cutting weight but are not prepared for the intensity of the workouts they will encounter at the next level.

By the time they become upperclassmen, those wrestlers who stick with the sport have, by and large, learned to adjust their diets and training to allow themselves to eat small, regular portions of food. But they don't dare go overboard, or they know they will have to pay the price.

At the time of McDonald's visit to Iowa, most of the Hawkeyes were intensely training for the nationals, which would take place in a few weeks at the Meadowlands in East Rutherford, N.J., and they were intensely managing their weight to ensure they would not be ruled too heavy to compete—"fat," as they called it, even though you would be hard-pressed to find a non-heavyweight Division I wrestler who had more than a few ounces of flab anywhere on his body.

Like the Hawkeyes, DeAnna was training, too, and dieting fiercely to make sure his weight would remain steady for the pre-Olympic competitions he faced in the coming weeks. He couldn't afford to let his energy levels drop, but he couldn't afford to take in anything extra, either.

And so, one afternoon after a workout at Carver-Hawkeye Arena, McDonald caught a ride with DeAnna and Baumgartner back to his hotel. Along the way, DeAnna stopped at a pharmacy, and the two wrestlers went inside to buy Gatorade. McDonald tagged along.

On the way back to their car, DeAnna stopped on the sidewalk and loosened the cap on the thirty-two-ounce bottle of sports drink he had just bought. Then, to McDonald's astonishment, DeAnna carefully poured exactly half of the bottle's contents— sixteen ounces—into a storm sewer. He took a sip, replaced the cap, and before getting into the car noticed McDonald looking at him, slack-jawed.

"He had this expression on his face like he had seen a big flying saucer land and a bunch of green aliens get out," DeAnna said. "I explained to him that I was cutting weight for the next competition, and I knew from experience that I could only drink sixteen ounces of fluids that night after practice to make sure I would be at the right weight the next morning.

"I knew if I left all the Gatorade in the bottle I would drink it, and I knew I couldn't afford to do that. So I dumped it in the street. To me and Bruce it was nothing out of the ordinary, but I don't think Mac had ever seen anything like that before in his life."

McDonald, the former basketball coach, had never encountered anything like these wrestlers. Their quirks and their diets and their seemingly endless training sessions made his head spin. In a matter of months, soon after their arrival at Edinboro to launch the athletic director's dream of a Division I wrestling program, DeAnna's and Baumgartner's heads would be spinning, too.

✦ ✦ ✦ ✦ ✦

OVER THE NEXT SEVERAL WEEKS, DeANNA AND BAUMGARTNER continued their quest for Olympic freestyle medals. DeAnna, twenty-six, fell short, unable to beat Lee Fullhart and Dave Schultz, two of the world's best wrestlers at his weight class. That put him on an awkward bubble. He needed to continue his training, without knowing if an injury or illness to a teammate might open a spot for him to compete at the Games. He was an unfortunate incident from realizing a lifelong dream of representing his country on amateur wrestling's biggest stage, and that dream never arrived.

Meanwhile, Baumgartner rolled through the Olympic Trials to clinch the top heavyweight spot on the U.S. team that would compete in Los Angeles in August. Even at twenty-four, a relatively young age in a sport whose masters often competed well past thirty, he was considered mature enough, athletic enough, and mentally tough enough to contend for the gold.

During their training sessions and on planes and buses to competition sites all over the country and even overseas, DeAnna and Baumgartner now had something else to think about. Back in Edinboro, Jim McDonald was preparing for their arrival. They knew they had enormous amounts of work to do to steel themselves for August, when the Olympics would be over and only a few short months would be left before Edinboro debuted its new program, with its pedigreed coaches and a promising young team that McDonald was quietly telling people around campus and around town could be capable of making some noise.

McDonald, of course, was feeding off his own optimism and off DeAnna's unsinkable enthusiasm. The former basketball coach had no real idea just how good Edinboro could be that season, and he would not be directly involved in shaping the lineup or training the Scots for what would prove to be the most pivotal season in the program's history.

But McDonald had plenty of other things to occupy his time, chief among them delivering on the promises he had made to DeAnna and Baumgartner the previous winter that everything they needed—a new weight room, locker rooms, an office suite— would go from budget line item to reality, if not in time for the start of the coming season then not long after that.

McDonald meant everything he said. He fully intended to fulfill every request his two young coaches had made, but the realities of a tight budget at a state-funded institution of higher education proved challenging, and when DeAnna and Baumgartner arrived—DeAnna as rambunctious teacher and promoter who had missed out on his chance to compete in Los Angeles but was determined to make his stamp as a coach; Baumgartner as conquering hero of the Olympic Games, winner of the first of his heavyweight gold medals (he would add another in 1992 to go along with a silver in 1988 and a bronze in 1996)— things were not quite as shiny and new as they had hoped.

The wrestling room—which had been the same for years— was dark and dingy. Little more than bare-bones funding had ever found its way to the program, and former coach Fred Caro had been forced to train his teams in Spartan conditions. The mats were ripped and they rested on a slab of cement because no one had ever come up with the money to build a suitable sub-floor to rest them on. The weight room was basically empty. The locker room didn't exist. The office suite consisted of a couple of pass-through rooms that were mostly treated as a hallway by fieldhouse inhabitants. When Baumgartner and DeAnna arrived, they went to their office and discovered a pair of universal weight machines on either side of what would serve as their desk for the first several weeks—a folding table with a bad set of legs that caused it to slope to one side.

Someone had strung a phone line through the open rafters above the room and dangled it onto the table. It was plugged into a single phone that DeAnna and Baumgartner would share, sliding it from one side of the slanted table to the other while making recruiting pitches and calls to Edinboro athletic boosters pleading for their money and support. The two men had just arrived from months of training at one of the Meccas of college wrestling—the University of Iowa, where the budget money flowed and Gable enjoyed all the support he needed to build and sustain a national powerhouse that was the envy of most every program in the land. Here in Edinboro, where they hoped to chase Gable's success, they were operating from a broken-down table with a single phone line atop folding metal chairs.

At least no one could say there wasn't some charm. In the steamy August heat, in the bowels of a hulking building with no air conditioning with the heat turned up to help the wrestlers lose weight, with bugs flitting around and landing on everything in sight, DeAnna and Baumgartner hung fly strips from the corners of their cockeyed table and took turns making calls from their single phone line to the people on whom the foundation of the program Jim McDonald envisioned as the "Iowa of the East" would be built.

| Chapter Five |

Early Returns

Mike Hahesy grew up in Ely, Iowa, a small town on the outskirts of Cedar Rapids that sprang up from the prairie when a German settler named Christopher Fuhrmeister bought a tract of fertile farmland and built a house for his wife and five children during the westward push of the 1840s.

By the time Hahesy was in grade school some 130 years later, Ely was still little more than a blip on the map with a population of 215, many of whom clung to their community's historic past amid the booming growth of the Cedar Rapids–Iowa City sector, which was marching toward the town on all sides.

The Iowa pheasant hunt, one of those local time-honored traditions, helped Hahesy find wrestling.

One morning when he was in the fifth grade, Hahesy went with a neighbor to the Cedar Rapids YMCA while his father, John, took the dogs out for some birding and his mother, Lynda, worked a shift at the local Hy-Vee grocery store.

Wrestling was on the activities schedule that morning at the YMCA, and Hahesy walked into a small gymnasium wide-eyed and watched kids rolling around on mats stretched across the floor. After a few minutes, he stepped out with them, a step that would change his future and shape his personal and professional lives forever.

Like many who stay with wrestling, Hahesy felt at home on the mats right away. By the time he was in seventh grade he was seeking out high school opponents to challenge him and force him to improve his technique. In 1981, he reached what is for some the pinnacle of Iowa high school sports when he won a Class AAA

Mike Hahesy, one of Mike DeAnna's original transfers from Division I powerhouse Iowa, was a Division II champion for Edinboro in 1985.

title at 145 pounds for Prairie High. The championship helped earn Hahesy a scholarship to the University of Iowa and a ticket to learn from Gable.

At Iowa, Hahesy became a super sub, a wrestler probably good enough to start for nearly any other program in the country, but not quite good enough to beat out the No. 1 wrestler at his weight class in his own practice room, three-time finalist and two-time NCAA champion Marty Kistler. By the end of his third year at Iowa, with two seasons of eligibility remaining, Hahesy decided to transfer rather than take the risk that he might never get a shot to start in a Hawkeyes program so rich with talent that some of it never managed to bubble to the surface.

Hahesy had done his research and settled on Cornell College, a small school in Mount Vernon, Iowa, whose wrestling program was nowhere near Iowa's level but where Hahesy could become a starter with a chance to make a couple of appearances at the nationals.

By the spring of 1984, Hahesy was set to leave for Cornell College—he had even picked out a roommate—when Gable approached him with an intriguing proposition. Would Hahesy be interested in following former Hawkeyes star Mike DeAnna to tiny Edinboro, Pennsylvania, to help build the foundation for an upstart Division I program that might someday produce wrestlers capable of challenging Iowa's?

"I had never heard of Edinboro," Hahesy later admitted. "But I had heard of Mike DeAnna."

DeAnna, Hahesy said, won him over with his outgoing personality, his love of the sport, and his willingness to work hard in the practice room. The two became fast friends as DeAnna trained for the Olympics and Hahesy put in hours waiting for the chance to crack the starting lineup. Once DeAnna started talking about his plans for Edinboro, Hahesy quickly became interested.

"You could go out and wash his car and you would feel real good about paying him twenty dollars to wash his car," Hahesy said of DeAnna years later. "That's how good of a salesman he was."

DeAnna had been good enough to sell Bruce Baumgartner on Edinboro. And at the time, Hahesy believed Baumgartner's name was on par with that of Olympic champion Dave Schultz's as the two biggest names in the sport. If this little program in the heart of the Lake Erie snow belt was good enough for DeAnna and Baumgartner, it was good enough for Hahesy.

Still, going to Edinboro was anything but an easy decision. Hahesy was the first member of his family to go to college. He had never been away from Iowa for any length of time. And he came from Ely, where, as he put it, "no one ever leaves." And now Gable was suggesting he uproot himself from his family and his home state and take his national championship aspirations east to a school where wrestling had always taken a backseat to basketball and football.

His final two years at Cornell College would have been free, and Hahesy's parents told him the only way he could go to Edinboro was if DeAnna could come up with enough money to make it free as well.

Done deal. DeAnna wanted Hahesy, knew he needed him, and McDonald—who had promised Hahesy during a visit to the school that he would have everything at Edinboro that he had at Iowa—was there to back up his coaches with the scholarship money they needed to land one of the biggest fish of Edinboro's first recruiting class under DeAnna and Baumgartner. Another Iowa backup with two seasons of eligibility remaining, Matt Furey, followed Hahesy to Edinboro, and the two became the only two non-freshmen on Edinboro's wrestling roster in the fall of 1984, a roster that would help the school launch itself into the college wrestling stratosphere, even if final ignition was still years from taking place.

In a few short weeks, Gable had watched one of his most accomplished former wrestlers and two talented current backups leave the Hawkeyes program for the promise of better things at a little school halfway across the country. He understood perfectly their reasons for leaving.

"You know, generally speaking the NCAA frowns on transfers," Gable said in recalling the departures of Hahesy and Furey and, a year later, two other Iowa wrestlers who found success at Edinboro, David Ray and Bob Kauffman. "But sometimes you have to look at what's best for the student-athlete. It wasn't that they didn't want to be at Iowa. They wanted the chance to compete.

"These were guys that knew they might be good enough to be national champions or All-Americans, but they weren't getting that chance. They wanted the opportunity to become bigger names in the sport, not just for their own good but to improve the sport and carry it on. They left for all the right reasons. They all made the right decision."

✤ ✤ ✤ ✤ ✤

B ACK IN EDINBORO AT THE END OF SUMMER, DEANNA AND Baumgartner had returned from the Olympics and were piecing together their team. Hahesy and Furey represented the foundation around which they added more than a dozen freshmen, some from the Cleveland area, where DeAnna had his roots and plenty of connections. Among them were Terry Kennedy, a high school standout from suburban Cleveland powerhouse Lakewood St. Edward; Kennedy's teammate, 177-pounder Dave Held; and little Dave Rowan, a 118-pound sparkplug from Madison, Ohio, along the southern shores of Lake Erie about halfway between Edinboro and Cleveland.

Years later, both DeAnna and Baumgartner acknowledged having rolled the dice by pegging their early success on transfers. Although DeAnna knew Hahesy and Furey, as well as David Ray and Bob Kauffman, there was always a risk with bringing in wrestlers who, for whatever reason, hadn't found success at their previous stops. For one thing, the program would be placed under the microscope by those who wondered what brand of athlete DeAnna and Baumgartner were bringing into the PSAC. And the expectations would be high. By landing talent from Gable's pipeline, Edinboro was placing a bull's eye on itself that the rest of the conference would aim for, on the mat and off. Already the new coaches had heard the murmurs from the state's other Division I teams. Someone somewhere had written that, in the new hierarchy of the PSAC wrestling world, there were now two havens—venerable Lock Haven and "Transfer Haven," the place Edinboro was fast becoming.

"We had sort of become the landing spot for—I don't want to use the word misfits, because a lot of times when kids transfer they transfer because they have a huge amount of baggage," Baumgartner said. "A lot of the kids we got, they just saw the light. They were maybe the second or third guy at their weight. They were unbelievably talented, but they were just that much behind.

"In basketball if you're just that much behind, you may get twenty minutes of playing time instead of thirty minutes. In wrestling it's usually either zero or all. Hahesy and Furey and Ray and Kauffman—they weren't kicked out of Iowa. They saw that they had one or two years left and they were the number two or three guy and they saw an opportunity."

Very soon, Hahesy and Furey became the program's first marketable names, and Kennedy, Rowan, and Held became its first homegrown stars. But first, DeAnna and Baumgartner needed to make it through the first season in the transition from Division II to Division I, a process that took two years and required a dramatic and nearly immediate upgrade in Edinboro's schedule.

The Baumgartners moved into the fixer-upper on Kinter Hill Road. The DeAnnas found a rental outside of Edinboro. The two coaches and their families were familiarizing themselves with the community and the campus, making connections they needed to help the fledgling Division I program get off the ground and sustain it beyond its first years. While working Edinboro's new wrestlers hard in the practice room twice a day, DeAnna and Baumgartner spent much of the rest of their time with McDonald cultivating relationships with new and existing boosters—"friends" of the athletic department, as McDonald liked to call them. One of the earliest and biggest of Edinboro's wrestling supporters was Cliff Troyer, whose family owned a potato chip company in nearby Waterford, a wrestling-crazed community that was at the time in its heyday under Coach Art Steves, a future member of the Pennsylvania Wrestling Hall of Fame. With supporters like Troyer endowing scholarships and providing vital sponsorship money to help DeAnna and Baumgartner get the program off the ground, the Division I wrestling dream was off to a solid start. But DeAnna had big plans, and they required much, much more of the salesmanship McDonald and Hahesy described.

Edinboro's first scheduled competition in the 1984–85 wrestling season was the West Virginia University Open in Morgantown. It provided a good early test for the Scots' freshman-heavy lineup, and it gave the two Iowa transfers—Hahesy and Furey—a chance to strut their Hawkeye-honed stuff. Furey was every bit as good as expected, winning the 167-pound championship and earning outstanding wrestler honors for the tournament. Three of Edinboro's freshmen—Kennedy, Held, and Dean Happel, a Lisbon, Iowa, native whom DeAnna landed from the shadow of Gable's Hawkeye machine in Lisbon—earned runner-up finishes in their collegiate debuts. Hahesy finished third, but it was obvious he was ready to join Furey as a Division II title contender.

Edinboro followed by winning the team championship at the Millersville Open in eastern Pennsylvania, where Hahesy won the

158-pound title. Rowan earned the outstanding wrestler award for his championship at 118. The Millersville tournament gave the Scots a chance to show off their new lineup in a field that included some of their PSAC rivals. But while the two tournaments gave DeAnna's wrestlers the chance to get up to speed on the road, much of the focus remained on the team's debut at McComb Fieldhouse against West Virginia, an event that DeAnna understood—long before his first schedule was finalized—would be much more than just a dual meet against an established Division I opponent. It was a once-in-a-lifetime, coming-out moment in front of the home fans, the athletic department's boosters, and the wrestling world in general, and the young coach was determined to make sure it was a party no one would soon forget.

DeAnna assigned many of the promotional duties to graduate Assistant Coach Gary Astorino, a former captain of Edinboro's wrestling team whose fifty-eight career wins ranked seventh in school history. Under direction from DeAnna and with the help of Edinboro's Scotties—Edinboro co-eds who served as volunteer support staff for every phase of the program in much the same way as Pam DeAnna had as a Mat Maid in Iowa—Astorino made up signs to resemble boxing posters billing Edinboro's home showdown against West Virginia. They stuffed them into the trunks and back seats of cars and delivered them all over, to schools, to stores—anywhere they might attract a crowd interested in watching Edinboro unveil its new look at home.

The posters were flashy and garish. They featured pictures of wrestlers in fierce poses with banner headlines reading, "Come see Matt 'The Mauler' Furey." They were designed to catch the eye of fans old and young alike, and they often wound up taped to walls in schools or stuck up beside scales in varsity wrestling rooms. DeAnna and Astorino had developed a database for sending out posters and promotional fliers for Edinboro's home matches, targeting fans based on the profile of the opponent and the significance of the match.

Pam DeAnna had by then, in a few short months, whipped the Scotties into shape. Drawing on her Mat Maid experience in Iowa, Pam made the Scotties study wrestling rule books and take quizzes—Mike DeAnna admitted he couldn't pass them—to prove they were fit to keep score during matches. She schooled them in supporting and promoting the program and dispatched them to distribute fliers and posters at local school cafeterias promoting Edinboro's wrestlers and home dual meets. The Scotties became an integral part of the program, one Jim McDonald didn't appreciate or understand at first.

The old-school McDonald, Mike DeAnna said, resisted the notion of putting "young girls" in charge of the scorebooks at the head table at McComb Fieldhouse. "I think he thought the only person at the scorer's table should be a forty-year-old man. But that's not the way college wrestling worked. I told him, 'Mac, you need to get out more.'"

But getting the word out and keeping score was only the start. DeAnna knew convincing local business to part with cold, hard cash to buy ads in the program or pay for billboards that would hang across the scorer's table at McComb Fieldhouse to support a still-obscure program would be a tough sell, so he was prepared to barter. He called a tuxedo rental place in Erie, the closest city about fifteen miles away, and asked for an ad. He was told the advertising budget was spent, a response he expected. He countered by asking for a free tuxedo rental in exchange for a small spot in the program and a promotional public address announcement during the West Virginia dual meet. Then he called a modeling agency in Erie. They, too, had exhausted their marketing budget. No problem. He worked out a deal for the agency to send over a few girls clad in swimsuits for the match.

"He hustled like no one I had ever seen in college athletics," McDonald said years later. "He was a born promoter."

By the night of the dual meet, DeAnna was ready to put on a show.

Two hours before the meet with the powerful Mountaineers began, DeAnna wandered into the McComb Fieldhouse and saw only two older men sitting in the bleachers, a couple of early arrivals who made the trip up from Morgantown to watch WVU. In the hallway outside the gym, McDonald joked with DeAnna, gesturing to the West Virginia fans and congratulating him on already breaking the previous year's single-match attendance mark.

But the fans began filing in, and within an hour McComb's wooden bleachers were bursting with a crowd of more than 2,500, a record for a home wrestling meet. Just before the first bout began, the lights went down, the smoke rolled out, and the spotlights came on. Paul Newman, Edinboro's sports information director, strode to the center of the mat in a top hat and tux with tails, holding a microphone and a card. Newman served as the "ring announcer" for the evening, and he introduced the wrestlers from each team with flashy nicknames—"In this corner, weighing 157 ¾ pounds, from Ely, Iowa . . . Mike 'Killer' Hahesy"—and stepped aside as the models, in their swimsuits, walked around the edge of the mat waving cards for each weight class.

McDonald and the school's president, Foster Diebold, joined DeAnna and Baumgartner on the Edinboro bench. While the two coaches screamed instructions and encouragement at their wrestlers, the two administrators took it all in with amazement. The Scots, still technically a Division II program, didn't win, although the dual meet against the Division I Mountaineers came down to the final two weight classes, which WVU won to take a 27–16 decision. But to DeAnna and McDonald, the night was an unqualified success.

"To tell you the truth, I never want to lose, ever," DeAnna said years later. "But at that point, with the status of the program and the place we were trying to get to, we were probably four years ahead of where anybody thought we would be on the very first day."

Later that night, long after the crowds had headed back home to talk about their first glimpse of big-time wrestling in little Edinboro, after the cleaning crews had picked up McComb, McDonald sought out his young coach to pass along a message. "That," the former basketball coach told Dan Gable's young disciple, "was the best sporting event that I've ever seen at Edinboro University."

There was plenty of work to be done. Neither DeAnna nor Baumgartner was satisfied with a respectable showing against an elite Division I team, even if Edinboro's lineup was nowhere near as good as it would be in a year or two, when the freshmen would be sophomores and juniors and more quality transfers would bolster the practice room. While this might have been the best wrestling Edinboro had ever seen, it was not close to the sort of wrestling DeAnna and Baumgartner were accustomed to being around. Even Hahesy, recalling those early months in the fall and winter of 1984, said the Scots "just weren't all that good—we had too many young guys." The season had just begun, and DeAnna was already squarely focused not only on the here and now and but also on the future. Still, as forward-thinking and restless as the former Hawkeye could be, even DeAnna admitted he paused briefly after the WVU dual meet to take satisfaction in how far the Scots had come since that seemingly ill-fated interview with McDonald several months earlier in the conference room at McComb Fieldhouse.

"My view of a wrestling program does not start and stop in the wrestling room," DeAnna said years later. "My view of a wrestling program is the complete picture—I'm talking about kids graduating, their GPAs. I'm talking about having people in the stands in support of the college and the program. And then the third part, not the first but the third, is what takes place in the wrestling room, including the student-athletes that are training there. The whole complete thing made our first dual meet a huge success. That was probably at the time the best team [West Virginia had ever fielded], and it came down to the last couple of matches.

"Those are the things I was thinking about in the interview. I think (McDonald) was just thinking, 'How do we beat Clarion?' But I was thinking, 'How do we get the gym packed? How do we get the good students? How do we get students who aren't in fights? How do we get the girls involved?' We didn't see eye-to-eye on everything, but I don't think anybody else could have done what Jim McDonald did. He saw some of the same things I saw, and he understood what I was trying to do. He had the vision, he had the energy, and he had the organizational skills. Without him, this never happens."

✦ ✦ ✦ ✦ ✦

Matt Furey, one of Edinboro's original transfers from the storied Iowa program. He and Mike Hahesy won NCAA Division II titles in Mike DeAnna's first year.

T HE SCOTS FOLLOWED THE WVU LOSS BY WINNING THREE straight duals against California (Pa.), Ohio University, and Youngstown State. The rest of the regular season was marked by peaks and valleys. Losses to Kent State and PSAC rival Lock Haven were softened by wins over Slippery Rock, Indiana (Pa.), and Toledo. Clarion beat Edinboro again, but this time the score was 30–17, and the Scots served notice that the days of the Golden Eagles practicing in McComb Fieldhouse's basement were long gone. Edinboro finished the season with a 7–6–1 dual meet record and prepared for its first postseason under DeAnna and Baumgartner, the month-long stretch that would prove just how far the two young coaches had brought their young team in a little less than a year's time.

Mike Hahesy

First up was the rugged PSAC tournament, where Edinboro finished fifth, its best showing in seven years. Then came the NCAA Division II Eastern Regional Championships at Pitt-Johnstown, near Pittsburgh. The Scots crowned five champions—Hahesy and Furey along with freshmen Kennedy, Held, and Brad Burkland, a heavyweight from East Moline, Illinois. Rowan reached the championship match before retiring with a separated shoulder that ended his season. The Scots claimed the tournament championship, the first in the program's history, and DeAnna was voted Eastern Region coach of the year by his peers. Hahesy and Furey followed by winning NCAA Division II national titles at Wright State University in Dayton, Ohio, leading Edinboro to a fifth-place finish, the school's highest ever. Under the rules at the time, the two qualified for the NCAA Division I nationals by reaching the Division II finals. *Amateur Wrestling News*, the sport's most respected publication, named DeAnna national rookie coach of the year.

Although Furey and Hahesy failed to place at the Division I nationals, they finished with records of 39–5–1 and 36–6–1 respectively, and freshman Dave Held went 31–15. The three moved into the top three spots on the program's single-season victories list.

Hahesy would use up his remaining eligibility the following year, coming up one match short of All-American status at the Division I tournament in Iowa City after suffering a one-point loss to Royce Alger, the blue-chip recruit who had replaced Marty Kistler at Iowa. Hahesy and Furey reached the Division II finals both years they were at Edinboro, and although each failed to realize his dream of a Division I medal, and while the Scots remained a step behind conference rivals Bloomsburg, Lock Haven, and Clarion, a sea change was at hand, and everyone in Edinboro's practice room sensed it.

"I think," Hahesy said years later, "we were able to help jump-start things for the program. Even though I didn't do what I went to Edinboro to do, which was win a Division I championship, I think we helped establish the tone in the room and in the program, and I think guys like Mike and Bruce and later Tim Flynn were able to benefit from that and carry it on."

With Furey's help, Hahesy had accelerated Edinboro's development with a work ethic and hard-nosed attitude that rubbed off on the first two groups of freshmen. Aided by McDonald's vision and budget, DeAnna and Baumgartner had transformed Edinboro in a matter of months from a neglected, underfunded Division II program into one capable of competing with the best teams in the country. As the first season wound down, DeAnna, the consummate salesman, headed out to meet with recruits bolstered by what his team accomplished. Now he had something to sell.

| Chapter Six |

Success and All Its Trimmings

WHILE A DRAMATIC TRANSFORMATION OF EDINBORO'S wrestling program was taking place on the mat, the new athletes Mike DeAnna and Bruce Baumgartner brought to the school were making their marks on the quiet little college town, too. By the end of the first year under DeAnna and Baumgartner, the wrestlers had developed a reputation for their constant workouts and single-minded focus on training themselves into shape to compete against the best opponents in Division I. In some cases, they also had developed reputations for their stamina at off-campus parties as well.

Some of the stories were too strange to be fiction, including reports of guns being shot in the air at parties and even an outlandish, but apparently true, tale of one wrestler who rode naked though the center of the college town on his motorcycle.

"One time my sister came to visit me at school and she stopped at the Hotel Bar to ask for directions," recalled Sean O'Day, Edinboro's first Division I champion and a leading advocate of the "train hard, have fun hard" lifestyle. "When the bartender found out who she was he told her to follow the trail of broken bottles. It was a crazy time. We were running 100 miles an hour with blinders on."

Jim McDonald often made somber visits to DeAnna's office in the basement of McComb Fieldhouse, plopped into the chair across from his young coach, and threatened to shut down the program if things didn't change. "I said, 'If I get another call from the police telling me they had to go into town and pull wrestlers off of bar stools or another call about a party they had to break up, I'm pulling the plug,'" McDonald recalled. "But he cleaned it up."

Hahesy's recollection is that it was nothing much worse than athletes mixing with beer, and he said the hardest of the partying didn't get into full swing until the second year of the program's rebirth.

DeAnna frequently had the wrestlers over to his house, where there was alcohol and trash talking and bruised egos and plenty of impromptu wrestling matches designed to settle an issue that carried over from the wrestling room or just blow off some steam. "It was a different time, twenty-some years ago," DeAnna recalled. "Today that never would have happened, but I was very young and I got so close to the kids so quickly. It really felt like we were all in this thing together."

Once, McDonald and another administrator, dressed in jackets and ties and with their wives in tow, dropped in for one of the get-togethers at DeAnna's house. The visitors barely made it through the front door when one of the young wrestlers spotted McDonald and moved in.

The former basketball coach might not have known much about wrestling, but he was fond of picking up tidbits about the strengths and weaknesses of certain wrestlers from the coaching staff and filing them away for future trash-talking purposes. McDonald had learned from DeAnna that this particular wrestler, an undersized freshman heavyweight from Strongsville, Ohio, named Erik Johnson, was weaker on his feet—in the neutral position—than he was on the mat. The truth was that Johnson had trained extensively in the Greco-Roman style, which emphasizes throws in favor of the usual leg attacks that are used in college matches. That nuance escaped McDonald, but it didn't keep him from routinely approaching Johnson during practices and riding him, asking incredulously, "Why don't you just grab his legs?"

That night at DeAnna's house, Johnson spotted McDonald

and ran at him, pinning him against one wall of the foyer. He lifted one of the athletic director's legs high in the air and shouted, "How do you like that Mr. McDonald? I've been taking your advice!" Thus ended that party.

At the NCAA tournament one year, McDonald was awakened by a call to his hotel room in the middle of the night. McDonald hung up the phone and scrambled downstairs to discover a shattered plate glass window outside one of the rooms that had been booked to Edinboro's wrestling team. A little asking around revealed that Dean Hall, a heavyweight who transferred from Oklahoma State during DeAnna's and Baumgartner's second year and would go on to become the program's first Division I finalist, had gotten into a wrestling match with 118-pounder Rob Porter. Hall, a gentle giant who weighed some 260 pounds, at one point picked up Porter and threw him through the window. McDonald could only shake his head and pay for the damages.

"It was the Wild West," Hahesy recalled. "That was kind of the motto at Iowa, too. You work hard and you have fun hard, too. I never remember anything bad, besides alcohol. The kids loved to party, but the next morning we had a 6 a.m. workout and everybody was there."

DeAnna didn't necessarily approve of such behavior, but he understood it. Few sports make the demands on an athlete's body that wrestling does, both with the constant training to exhaustion and the constant pressure to lose weight. The stress could be unimaginable, and sometimes the best way to deal with it was to escape reality for awhile. Like Gable in Iowa, DeAnna told his wrestlers to keep up their class work, deal with their demons the best way they could, and make sure they showed up ready to wrestle once they stepped in the room.

"You could do whatever you wanted to do as long as it didn't affect you here (in the practice room)," Hahesy recalled. "If it affected you here, then you had to change your habits." That was one of the reasons DeAnna and his wrestlers became such a tight-knit bunch so fast, why they trusted him so completely when he explained the lengths they would need to go to achieve greatness.

Just as Gable had constantly referred to his "family" of

thirty-five wrestlers in the Hawkeyes program, DeAnna was quickly growing close to his wrestlers at Edinboro. They were a mismatched group right from the start, composed of castoffs, forgotten high school stars, overlooked prospects, or wrestlers who simply needed a chance to prove themselves.

And Mike Hahesy was their ringleader. He was the one who most thoroughly tormented his coaches, especially Baumgartner.

Even as a heavyweight, Baumgartner closely watched his diet. He didn't drink, and one of his only vices was the occasional Kit Kat candy bar. During his first years at Edinboro, when he was still competing heavily, Baumgartner would stuff Kit Kats into his gym bag and nibble on them at the end of his workouts. It was a small reward for the hours of brutal training. Word spread quickly, and before long the treats started to come up missing.

"We would steal them and hide them, and he would come back into the locker room looking for them and just be furious," Hahsey recalled. "He would call everyone in and line us up, go from guy to guy like a drill sergeant, trying to figure out who took his Kit Kats. You just stood there and tried really hard not to laugh."

At tournaments, Hahesy would scan the crowd for the biggest, sloppiest fat guy he could find. Then, with an audience of teammates stifling their giggles, he would call over Baumgartner.

"Hey Bruce, there he is!" Hahesy would say excitedly, pointing toward the fat guy.

"Who?" Baumgartner would reply.

"Right there! That's the guy that beat you at states your senior year in high school! Boy, it's hard to believe you lost to a guy that looks like that. He's really let himself go, hasn't he?"

Despite their hijinks and occasional misbehavior, Hahesy and the rest of those early recruits had immense talent. They came together almost immediately and became very close. They quickly grew on their coaches, who loved their work ethic and their willingness to do anything DeAnna and Baumgartner told them to do, right down to the most perversely difficult drills and training regimens. DeAnna was amused by their naivety and their curiosity about Edinboro, the small town and small school which for most of them did not exist until they heard the name roll off of DeAnna's tongue during a recruiting call.

During his first team meeting at the start of the school year in the fall of 1984, DeAnna had gathered the incoming Scots in a classroom in McComb Fieldhouse. He gave them an impassioned speech in which he told them that he had never learned to accept losing, and that anyone who did would have to be labeled a loser. He made it clear that he was there, as were they, to turn Edinboro into a powerhouse. He drew on the best stuff he could recall from Gable's frequent motivational talks and tried his best to help them get caught up in the excitement of their new school and the opportunities it presented to make a name for themselves for the revamped program on the national scene. Then he paused, caught his breath, and asked if there were any questions. The room seemed tense, with many of the young wrestlers still processing what DeAnna had said. This was business, they realized. This was what it was going to be like to wrestle with heavy expectations beneath the demands of an intense, driven coach. You could have heard a tissue drop.

Then, from a desk in the back, Matt Furey, the prematurely balding transfer from Iowa, raised his hand. "I heard that we have to wear singlets that say 'Boro' on them—is that true?" Furey asked, referring to the shortened version of the school's name popularized by students, only mispronouncing it "borrow."

DeAnna laughed. These were his wrestlers, for better or worse.

✤ ✤ ✤ ✤ ✤

INTO THE TRAIN-HARD, HAVE-FUN-HARD ATMOSPHERE TAKING root in the basement of McComb Fieldhouse, DeAnna and Baumgartner launched into Year Two with another strong recruiting class headed by three more transfers from big-name programs.

Hall, a pinning machine who had recorded seventy of his seventy-eight wins by fall during high school in Fruita, Colorado, arrived from powerful Oklahoma State, where he had gone 21–11 for the Cowboys as a redshirt freshman. The 260-pound Hall

Heavyweight Dean Hall, Edinboro's first
Division I finalist, in an undated university
publicity photo.

was in the Baumgartner mold of big, strong heavyweights who
could move, and he would become the newly crowned Olympic
champion's personal project for the next three seasons.

DeAnna also returned to Iowa and plucked two more wrestlers
from Gable's stable of backups, lightweight David Ray and
middleweight Bob Kauffman, who, like Hahesy and Furey, were
expected to win right away. As a bonus, the Scots got Greg Wright,
a senior from the Cleveland area whom DeAnna had brought in
during his first season but who was ineligible to compete.

Now, with a lineup that included a pair of returning Division
II champions in Hahesy and Furey, three more well-trained
transfers in Hall, Ray, and Kauffman, and the development of
the sophomores from that first recruiting class, DeAnna believed
Edinboro was on the verge of taking its next big next steps. To

DeAnna, that meant two things—beefing up the Scots' schedule to include the biggest names in the sport, and putting an Edinboro wrestler on top of the medal stand at the NCAA Division I nationals.

The first part didn't take too long. Again tapping into his former coach's love for the sport and desire to promote it, DeAnna convinced Gable to put Edinboro on his schedule for the 1985–86 season. Although Iowa pounded the Scots 40–7, the dual meet was competitive enough to lead to meetings the next two seasons, including one of the major accomplishments of the DeAnna-Baumgartner era, Gable's agreeing to bring his Hawkeyes to McComb Fieldhouse for a dual meet in December 1988. Todd Jay, who replaced Paul Newman as sports information director at the start of DeAnna's second season, later described the match as "just an unbelievable coup for the program." As big as the West Virginia dual meet had been a few years earlier, this was on an entirely different level. Iowa was far and away the dominant team in the country, the defending national champion, and a program whose mystique and tradition followed it wherever it traveled.

The result was a 23–12 Iowa win, not that the result was important. The Hawkeyes' presence in McComb Fieldhouse, the sight of their black and yellow warm-ups and of Gable barking orders to them from a chair on his side of the mat was enough to drive home the point. McComb was, Jay recalled years later, "packed to the rafters." There were fans seated on the floor all around the mats. Edinboro had arrived at the apex of college wrestling. In just two years at the Division I level, DeAnna and Baumgartner had the Scots competing head-to-head, on their own mats, with Dan Gable's Iowa Hawkeyes, and some of them were winning. There was no question they were on the right path.

The second big step, that first NCAA Division I champ, wasn't far behind. In fact, unbeknownst to DeAnna and Baumgartner in the fall of 1985, he was tucked away in the program's second recruiting class, a fiery freshman from just up the road whose nickname, "Bomber," only hinted at the impression he would leave on Edinboro by the time his four seasons on the mat were done.

Sean O'Day arrived with unimpeachable credentials. He

won a Pennsylvania Interscholastic Athletic Association (PIAA) championship at Meadville Area Senior High School, one of the state's top programs. He was a champion at 132 pounds in the state's largest classification for wrestling, having capped a career that included 148 high school wins with a 36–0 senior season. He possessed incredible speed and was superbly conditioned, two things that would translate as he transitioned from high school to college. There were things DeAnna and Baumgartner could teach. They could improve a wrestler's technique, make him stronger, sharpen his mental focus, and show him how to minimize his weaknesses. But there were qualities the great ones tended to share—chief among them natural wrestling ability and killer instinct—and O'Day had quantities of both to spare. It's why he had been recruited by two of the biggest Division I programs in the country—Nebraska and Penn State—before deciding to stay close to home and train under DeAnna and Baumgartner, and with the Iowa transfers, at a school just twenty minutes from his hometown.

Three things stood out from the black-and-white publicity photograph of O'Day that appeared on page thirteen of Edinboro University's 1985–86 wrestling media guide. There, between photos and short bios for David Ray and Greg Wright, was a mugshot of O'Day, his body turned to his right, his head looking at a slight angle toward the camera. He wore a plaid jacket of indiscernible color, and his blond hair, almost white, faded into the bright sky in the background of the photo, which was snapped outside McComb Fieldhouse. But the most striking part of the photo was O'Day's eyes, narrow and piercing, belying no fear, and giving him the look of someone who knew something you didn't.

At the time of the photo, O'Day was still just another great high school wrestler who had yet to prove a thing on the college mats. The sport is littered with athletes who peaked early, winning championships in high school or even as pre-teens, only to fail to match that success when they reached college. There is no shortage of theories on why this happens. Some wrestling people believe that kids who win at a young age simply run out of reasons to prove themselves when they get older. Others believe years of nearly non-stop, intense training and dieting, of putting the body back together again after the season in just a few short weeks before offseason workouts begin, takes too steep a toll.

One of O'Day's contemporaries, a wrestler named Rodney Wright from nearby Lakeview High School, won three PIAA championships and was one of the gems of Edinboro's 1987 recruiting class, but he lost his only match the only year he qualified for the nationals in 1990. In the world of Division I wrestling recruiting, even among the best of the best, there were no sure things. The plan for O'Day was for him to redshirt his first season to acclimate himself to the college scene, then make a push the following year. A quote from DeAnna, which illustrated how hopeful Edinboro's coaches were that he could develop into something special, accompanied O'Day's bio in the wrestling media guide: "Sean's a blue-chipper who will return after this year with four years of eligibility remaining," the quote began. "He is a physical specimen who will become more deadly with every move he learns."

As far as DeAnna and Baumgartner were concerned, O'Day possessed enormous upside. Not only did he have talent, but he was also a local kid who could draw crowds from the communities around Edinboro who had watched him grow up dominating the competition at Meadville. As talented as he was, he was still raw, which meant DeAnna and Baumgartner could mold him into the sort of wrestler who would prove the new coaching staff knew how to find talent and develop it.

In the fall of 1985, a visitor to Edinboro's practice room could have looked around and spotted any number of candidates to break through and become the first home-grown talent to deliver the national championship that Jim McDonald had dreamed of when he made that call to Dan Gable in a fit of anger a year and a half earlier.

There was sophomore Dave Rowan, the little 118-pound sparkplug, who might have won at least one NCAA title for the Scots had he not battled injury after injury throughout his career. There was Terry Kennedy, the sophomore from North Olmstead, Ohio, who became a two-time All-American and established the school record for career wins. There was Dave Held, who set a freshman record with thirty-one wins in 1984–85 and later became a two-time Division II place-winner. There was Rob Porter, the Illinois state champ who, like Rowan, Kennedy, and Held, was one of DeAnna's and Baumgartner's first freshmen, and who won eighty-three career college matches but, for all his talent, never found his way onto the medal stand at the nationals. There were freshmen like Dan Willaman from North Canton, Ohio; twins Erik and Craig Christensen from nearby Erie; and Michael Chupak, a Pennsylvania state champ from tiny Hadley, half an hour from Edinboro. And there was Sean O'Day, with the white-blond hair and laser-beam eyes, who perhaps possessed more quickness and potential than anyone else in the room, but who, by the very nature of the sport, was no more a lock to be great than any of them.

|Chapter Seven|

O'Day

O NE OF THE DEFINING MOMENTS OF THE DEANNA-BAUMGARTNER era came in 1987, when Dean Hall became the first Edinboro wrestler to compete for a Division I title by reaching the heavyweight final at that year's tournament in College Park, Maryland.

Hall finished second, losing 4–2 to Pitt-Johnstown's Carlton Haselrig, a ridiculously athletic heavyweight who would go on to play four seasons as an NFL lineman, including three with the Pittsburgh Steelers, despite not playing football in college.

Hall's finals appearance was a tremendous boost for the program. It put the Scots in the national spotlight and held up DeAnna and Baumgartner as coaches capable of steering talent through the potholes of the NCAA tournament bracket.

But it came with an asterisk.

"When Hall made the final it was huge," Baumgartner said. "But it was still a transfer."

Even though he spent three seasons at Edinboro and placed in the top four at the Division I nationals each year, Hall was regarded as Oklahoma State property, a second-hand star. Despite Hall's success, DeAnna and Baumgartner knew they needed to put one of their own wrestlers—one they recruited and signed and trained from scratch—atop the medal stand at the nationals before they could prove to the world, and just as importantly to themselves, that they had arrived on the major college wrestling scene.

Sean O'Day, who won Edinboro's first
NCAA Division I title in 1989, in an undated
university publicity photo.

ONE OF THE BEST THINGS THAT EVER HAPPENED TO EDINBORO
wrestling might have been a loss by Sean O'Day that didn't count
against any official record. Just days after O'Day won the Class
AAA 132-pound title as a senior at Meadville High School,
he was pitted against that year's Class AA champion in an all-
star match the weekend after the PIAA tournament. O'Day's
opponent was Derrick Hall of Jeannette High School, a small
school from a hardscrabble town in the coal-streaked highlands
outside Pittsburgh. No one expected Hall to have much of a shot
against O'Day, least of all the two schools that had been courting
the Meadville star—Penn State and Nebraska. But when Hall
pulled one of the match's biggest upsets, suddenly DeAnna and
Baumgartner had a chance.

No one knows for sure how serious the bigger schools were about O'Day before the loss. O'Day recalled years later that neither Penn State nor Nebraska had made a firm financial commitment. His parents, driven by working class sensibilities, were sold on a scholarship offer made by DeAnna and Baumgartner, and on the fact that Sean would be twenty minutes away.

"We were down to the wire as far as signing dates and money were concerned, and my parents were worried," O'Day recalled. "I came home from school one day and they said, 'We've thought about it, and you're going to Edinboro.' It really wasn't my decision."

DeAnna, meanwhile, was convinced the bigger schools backed off following O'Day's loss. He and Edinboro moved in, landing an unusually gifted prospect at the cost of three-quarters of a scholarship. It proved to be some of the best bargain hunting of DeAnna's career. "If that loss in the all-star match hadn't happened, we would never have had a shot at Sean," DeAnna recalled. "We should have sent that kid from Jeannette an Edinboro wresting jacket."

The initial plan was to red-shirt O'Day to allow his body to fill out and give him the chance to hone his technique in the practice room for a season before turning him loose to pursue a national medal. He sat out the first two months of competition, going through the daily training sessions but sitting in the stands for matches and tournaments.

But DeAnna and Baumgartner soon changed their minds.

There was pressure from McDonald, who had fought to fully fund the program with $40,000 in scholarship money. The athletic director had trouble accepting that a prized recruit was, as DeAnna put it, "running around McComb Fieldhouse wearing gym shorts" while the Scots were forfeiting his weight class as Greg Wright worked to regain his eligibility. There was pressure from fans who showed up for home dual meets expecting to watch O'Day, the local kid, take on the best competition in the country.

Fortunately, the coaches felt O'Day was ready—as ready as he could be, at least. Unlike Hahesy, Furey, Kennedy, and some of the other wrestlers they had trained, O'Day's game was not about strength and size and wearing out an opponent with muscle and pressure. O'Day's game was pure speed and explosiveness, and it was unlikely a year of limited competition was going to do him much good. "People can debate whether or not we should have red-shirted him," Baumgartner said. "But the thing we recognized with Sean was that he had the talent and the ability, he just needed the polish, and that was going to come on the mat against really good competition."

That meant throwing the eighteen-year-old O'Day, still a boy for all practical purposes, into the fire against fifth-year seniors who were twenty-three-year-old men. It meant accepting losses—in some cases against wrestlers with less natural ability but more moxie and strength—losses that were going to wear on the young star and lead DeAnna and Baumgartner to wonder then and later if they had made the right decision.

After the coaches put O'Day into the lineup in January and February, the setbacks came early and often. DeAnna and Baumgartner had become frustrated with O'Day, not because of his effort, which was admirable for a true freshman, but because neither of them could quite figure out what it would take to coax his talent from him and help him perform at the level he had in high school.

"His first year he didn't know what it took," Baumgartner said. "You put them in there, they take their lumps, they get beat up, they get beat out, and then you have a list of things you need to fix. Sean was a pretty hard worker, but I think that first year or two we worked the wrong way."

O'Day went 7–7 in January and February, far less than a glimmering start to his wildly anticipated college career. But the coaches were eager to see him get the chance to compete in the postseason, to see what would happen when his competitive juices began to flow.

In late February, a couple of weeks before the East Region championships—the national qualifying tournament that decided who advanced to pursue an NCAA title—DeAnna and Baumgartner scheduled a wrestle-off for the 142-pound weight class between O'Day and Wright, the transfer from Cleveland

State who had been sitting out. The winner would be the starter; the loser would be done until next year, at least competitively, but would be expected to remain in the practice room and serve as a drilling partner to help the other one prepare for a postseason run.

O'Day and Wright had been within a point or two of each other in countless matches in the practice room that winter, and the coaches expected a competitive battle that either wrestler had a chance to win. So imagine how stunned they were when Wright scored a quick takedown, slapped a spiral half on O'Day, and pinned the promising freshman about a minute into their match.

That quickly, O'Day's season was over, burned up with no chance of a red-shirt and no opportunity to wrestle in the postseason. Even twenty-five years later, having won a national championship and having earned induction into the Eastern Wrestling League hall of fame, O'Day stews over the decision to pull him from his redshirt year. He fought it then, and he would fight it again. "I lost a year because they wanted me in the lineup so we could win a dual meet against Clarion," O'Day recalled. "They pulled me aside and gave me the speech. They said it was best for me and that it would help the team. But I didn't want to hear them talk. After that, I always felt after that like they owed me something."

The wisdom of DeAnna's and Baumgartner's decision would be debated for months. But one thing was clear: While there had been glimpses of O'Day's ability, by the end of his first season there was still much more talent trapped inside him than anyone had seen from him while wearing a singlet with "Boro" printed across the front.

Finally, as O'Day's sophomore season approached, DeAnna and Baumgartner hit upon something they thought was worth trying. Just as O'Day's wrestling style was in stark contrast to Hahesy's or Furey's or Kennedy's, his training needed to be different, too. He was a different breed of recruit, and his body reacted to Edinboro's workout regimen differently than most of the team's other wrestlers.

Baumgartner explained years later:

In wrestling, we're not all the same. What might build me up might tear you down. You can't take a kid and try to mold him into your training system just because it works for someone else. What we found with Sean was that we had to train him differently than most of the other kids. A kid like a Hahesy or a Tony Robie or a Jason Robison or a Josh Koscheck needed that physicality every day. They needed to go to war in the practice room and beat on somebody or they felt like they hadn't accomplished anything.

Sean couldn't do that. His body would wear down. Where the other kids might wrestle for an hour and ride the bike for thirty minutes, we might have Sean wrestle for twenty minutes and ride the bike for an hour. It took us a long time, pretty much two full years, to figure out what would work for him, and when we figured it out that's when he started to win.

There was something else, too, something that would lead DeAnna, nearly twenty years after O'Day won Edinboro's first Division I title, to describe him as "the most difficult kid to coach I ever had." It wasn't meant as a slight. O'Day had been accustomed to competing at an extraordinarily high level coming out of Meadville's legendary practice room. Meadville's schedule was so tough that he had already faced much of the state's best competition even before the postseason began, and even if he hadn't faced them during the season, he had probably drilled or competed against those elite opponents during offseason club practices or tournaments. O'Day knew how to win, knew exactly how to react in almost any situation in a match against almost any opponent attacking him with almost any style. He was, in his own words, "a pain in the ass."

"My attitude was you're not going to tell me what to do," O'Day said. "I'm going to tell you."

O'Day was, as DeAnna would later say, "like a thoroughbred horse." That both excited Edinboro's coaches and frustrated them to no end.

"You want kids like Sean because they're so talented," DeAnna recalled. "But at the same time it's so difficult to change them. When they get into a situation in a match where it's do or die, when there's fifteen seconds to go and they're down by a point and they need to do something to win, they're going to go back to that move that got them there. No matter how much you train them in the practice room to do some other move that you want them to do in that situation, when it comes down to crunch time they're going to do what feels natural."

It meant that 90 percent of the time O'Day's talent was superior enough to allow him to win. But the other 10 percent of the time, when he ran into an opponent who knew how to stop his best moves, who knew how O'Day would react when do or die time arrived, he would have to come up with something new. And that marked O'Day's first three years at Edinboro. He enjoyed plenty of success, finishing seventh at the nationals as a sophomore in 1987 and second in 1988, but each time he ran into an opponent who stopped his best stuff when it counted most. In the 142-pound finals at the nationals in 1988, Pitt's top-seeded Pat Santoro beat O'Day 16–11, a loss that completely changed O'Day's approach to his final college season.

Santoro was a junior when he beat O'Day in the 1988 finals, and he would be back, stronger than ever, to try to defend the title in 1989. O'Day had the speed and explosiveness to hang with anyone in the country, but Santoro was able to grind away and stop his signature move—a lightning-quick ankle pick—at the most critical times.

DeAnna and Baumgartner were convinced O'Day's best shot would be at 134 pounds, meaning he would have to cut eight more pounds off of a body that was carrying precious little extra weight to begin with. That would be the cost of winning a national title, they said.

O'Day fought them every step of the way. For starters, he believed he could beat Santoro, and the last thing he wanted was for anyone to suggest he was ducking him. He reacted with anger and frustration, much the same way he felt as a freshman when the coaches pulled him off his redshirt year.

"I ran away for a while and just didn't want to hear them talk," O'Day recalled years later. "In the practice room I would just starting beating up on people because I was mad about what was going on. Pretty soon Bruce would come over and say, 'Okay, here we go.' And he would take me out in the hallway and have me do something to punish me, like carry a 300-pound stack of weights all the way to the top of the stairs and back down. But that kind of backfired, because I liked doing that stuff. And if I could show them it didn't bother me, then I felt like I won."

It was an epic battle between an athlete and his coaches, and eventually O'Day acquiesced. Early in the fall of his senior year, O'Day, DeAnna, and Baumgartner went to work devising a training regimen that would turn him into a national champ. "I swear," O'Day recalled, "DeAnna would lie awake nights dreaming up s--t for me to do."

Even at 134 pounds, it would not come easily. O'Day lost five times during the regular season his senior year and entered as the third seed for that year's nationals, which were held at the Myriad Center in downtown Oklahoma City, in the shadow of national power Oklahoma State. The seeding was a slight, O'Day believed, for a wrestler who had been a runner-up at a higher weight class the year before. More importantly, it meant he would have to wrestle an extra match, starting in the sixteen-man pigtail round, to return to the national final.

"I was upset I got the seed that I got at the start," O'Day told his hometown newspaper, *The Meadville Tribune*, in an account of the tournament that appeared a few days later. "It really upset me that here I was a national runner-up at a higher weight class and I was the third seed and had to wrestle in the pigtails. But in the long run, though, it worked out in my favor. When I saw the chart, I knew I got the best draw of all the top seeds. So in that respect they did me a favor."

O'Day won his first two matches by technical fall and his next two by major decision to reach the semifinals. The ankle pick was nearly unstoppable, and he was on top of his game heading into a showdown against second-seeded Joe Melchiore of Iowa, a classic brawler known for his dangerous throws. The talk before the match was about whether O'Day could keep from getting launched by the Gable-trained Hawkeye. But O'Day didn't buy it. He told the *Tribune* later that he spent the hours before the match planning how he would control Melchiore, how he would force the Iowa wrestler into his style, how he would take him out of his comfort zone. It worked. Not only did O'Day keep from getting launched, he threw Melchiore to his back twice in an 8–3 win that sent him soaring back to the national final.

On the other side of the bracket, the news was even better. Michigan's John Fischer, the top seed and a wrestler whose style might have given O'Day problems, was upset by fourth-seeded T. J. Sewell of Oklahoma. At that point, O'Day could not have been more confident, saying later, "To tell the truth, after that match I thought I had already won the national championship."

DeAnna felt like he was floating through the Myriad Center on some whispy cloud, too. He doubted Gable's Hawkeye sensibilities would permit the Iowa coach to agree with him, but in DeAnna's mind O'Day had "beaten the crap out of Melchiore." The home-grown Edinboro kid—not a transfer, not a second-hand talent—had beaten the Iowa kid in the national semifinals. For all the respect DeAnna had for Gable, this felt sweet. It could only be sweeter if O'Day won the whole thing.

Right there in Oklahoma City on cable TV—ESPN televised that year's finals—O'Day gave up the first takedown to Sewell, then took the Oklahoma wrestler down twice in the second period to lead 8–6 entering the final two minutes of the match. O'Day escaped for a point, then finished with another ankle pick, a takedown that sealed an 11–8 win that put him atop the medal stand at the nationals and provided a lot of peace of mind.

"It felt like a huge weight had been lifted off my shoulders," O'Day recalled nearly two decades after winning the title. "You put so much effort into something and you want it to happen. If it doesn't, you carry that burden forever."

It never came to that. Thanks to O'Day and the coaches he had hand-picked only four years earlier, Jim McDonald had the national champion he coveted, even if he could barely watch O'Day's crowning moment. Years later, McDonald admitted his stomach was turning as he sat in the stands during the final. Todd Jay, Edinboro's sports information director, said he glanced at McDonald several times, "and all I kept seeing was his bald head and his face in his hands. He was too nervous to watch. He was too afraid of what might happen if Sean lost."

More than twenty years later, DeAnna insists he did not need O'Day's title to validate in his own mind that Edinboro had arrived. "It was probably a bigger accomplishment for the university and its reputation than for me and Sean personally," he recalled. "I didn't need that, but the recruits probably needed it. I believed in us already. I guess I always thought that our kids were going to get their hands raised every time."

Nonetheless, DeAnna knew he could not downplay what it meant to the program. The title, along with Terry Kennedy's seventh-place finish and an eighth by Frank Zelinsky, vaulted Edinboro past Penn State and into ninth place in the team standings. It wasn't the Scots' highest finish at the nationals under DeAnna and Baumgartner, but it was the first time they had finished as the highest scoring team from the Eastern United States.

They had, indeed, become the Iowa of the East. And even DeAnna allowed that meant something. "I'd say," he said, "we came close to doing the impossible."

Looking back, Baumgartner said, O'Day's national championship might have been the single most important accomplishment of the DeAnna era, not just for what it meant at the time, but what it meant for the next two decades. O'Day's title established Edinboro as a place where raw, untested prospects could develop into polished champions. It opened doors that had closed on DeAnna and Baumgartner in previous years. It brought them wrestlers who had turned up their noses before.

"The one that made the biggest impact was Sean O'Day," Baumgartner recalled. "He was our first four-year national champion, and that showed the Lou Rossellis of the world, the Tony Robies of the world, the Jason Robisons, the Kevin Sanigas—hey, Baumgartner and DeAnna, they can coach. When you take someone else's property it's a little different. Now, instead of getting the one-time state placer or maybe one-time champ who might develop into something good someday, we were able to get the Rossellis, who were pretty good bets to be successful."

|Chapter Eight|

Transitions

IF THE ARRIVALS OF MIKE DEANNA AND BRUCE BAUMGARTNER put Edinboro wrestling on the map, then Sean O'Day's national championship helped it go from a small, lightface outpost to a bold, fully blown crossroads for college wrestling talent. Just as Baumgartner had hoped, O'Day's success gave the program much-needed credibility by demonstrating that the two coaches could not only successfully shout instructions from the corner at wrestlers groomed at the big-time schools, but they also could find talented young prospects and turn them into winners. Although plenty of people every year at the nationals still look bewildered and ask, "Where's Edinboro?" the school gained instant name recognition among the most influential people in the sport—coaches and wrestlers at both the college and high school levels. Edinboro joined a relatively small fraternity of programs that could say it produced a wrestler better than any other in the country at that particular weight that particular season. In that sense, DeAnna and Baumgartner had done what Gable so routinely did at Iowa, mold a champion from the promising raw materials of an untested recruit.

But even in the wake of O'Day's momentous achievement, the program was beginning to stutter. Baumgartner and DeAnna were still putting in long days and nights coaching and scouring for recruits, but Baumgartner had resumed his training in earnest in preparation for making a run at the gold medal in the 1992 Olympics in Barcelona, Spain, and DeAnna had become interested—and heavily invested—in a side venture selling wrestling shoes. By Baumgartner's own admission, the

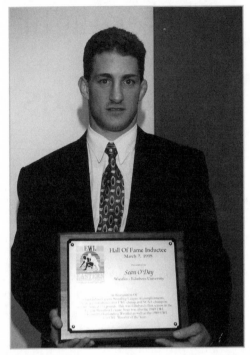

Sean O'Day, Edinboro's first NCAA Division I champion, poses with a plaque marking his induction into the Eastern Wrestling League hall of fame in 1998.

1989–90 recruiting class—the one that immediately followed O'Day's title—was the worst the two produced in their six seasons together. Few of the wrestlers from that group graduated, and many of them brought what Baumgartner called "a lot of extra baggage that really made it tough for them to be successful." There was still some incredible talent in the room, including a second-year wrestler named Lou Rosselli who became one of the most important names in the program's history as a two-time All-American, assistant coach, and 1996 Olympian. But after finishing eighth, seventh, and ninth at the nationals in their first three seasons at the Division I level, the Scots slid to a disappointing forty-third in 1989–90 and had no All-Americans—one of only three times from 1986 through 2007 that the program failed to put a wrester on the NCAA medal stand.

The two men poured their hearts and souls into Edinboro

wrestling. Not long after they arrived and discovered that the mats in the wrestling room were stretched across cement floors in the basement of McComb Fieldhouse—a cold, damp combination that was neither safe nor conducive to training elite athletes—Baumgartner and DeAnna brought in the wrestlers on a Saturday for a construction project. Because of union rules at the state-run school that would have tied up the project indefinitely in red tape and purchase orders, they worked in secret and completed the job before anyone noticed. Using donated lumber and Baumgartner's carpentry skills, they built a sub-floor for the mats and stretched them back out by the end of the day. Baumgartner later helped build the wood-framed lockers in the new wrestling locker room that occupied roughly the same spot as that broken-down desk with the fly strips had a couple of years earlier.

Together, DeAnna and Baumgartner recruited their wrestlers, trained with them, bled with them, shed tears with them, and, in DeAnna's case, at least, drank beers with them. They argued over who would, as Baumgartner put it, "play coach" and who got to stand in as de facto drill partner during practices, because each still preferred to be on the mat with the kids, not running the timer and carrying the whistle.

"To get where we needed to get as fast as we wanted to get there it was a 24/7 thing," DeAnna said years later. "I was their teammate as much as I was their coach, and I think it was the same for Bruce. We were doing everything, because when we got there we felt like the only way we could do it was all wrestling, all the time."

The pace took its toll on DeAnna, whose kids were growing up. His son Tony, who turned seven in 1989, was showing interest in wrestling. DeAnna did not want to be stuck on planes or buses or marooned in faraway arenas while his son cut his teeth in the sport. There was also the shoe business, which was growing and for which DeAnna had big plans. And, of course, there was the one thing that continued to gnaw at DeAnna, even after the three straight top-ten finishes at the nationals and O'Day's magical trip through the 134-pound NCAA bracket in March 1989: the constant challenge to prove that Edinboro was a top-tier wrestling program.

When DeAnna had been at Iowa serving as Gable's recruiting coordinator, he never fully appreciated how redundant his position had been. Years later he recalled how he would scan a list of high school wrestlers, pick up the phone and say, "Hello, you want to wrestle for Gable?"

In the world of high-stakes high school and college wrestling, those words were the ultimate icebreaker. DeAnna recalled receiving countless letters from top-notch wrestlers from everywhere in the country begging to come to Iowa City and train under the best coach the sport had ever known.

"It was the easiest job I ever had in my life," DeAnna said.

Edinboro was nothing like that. To get Mike Hahesy and Matt Furey to agree to wrestle for him that first year he had to offer them full scholarships—full scholarships for backup wrestlers who had failed to even qualify for the nationals one time! To land Kennedy and Rowan, he had to ante up full rides for wrestlers who, though talented, had never even won the Ohio state high school tournament. It had been all he could do to convince Mike Flynn, an above-average competitor but more grinder than superstar at Davenport Assumption High School in Iowa, where DeAnna coached while working for Gable, to join him in Edinboro. And Flynn remained angry for a long time because DeAnna would not give him a full ride. Even some of his closest friends and training partners had sniffed when he asked if they might be interested in helping him coach. "Nobody wanted to come," DeAnna recalled. And while things improved after the Scots enjoyed some early success, selling Edinboro wrestling remained an awesome challenge.

Even four years after DeAnna and Baumgartner had arrived, it was not uncommon for a recruiting call to abruptly end with a high school wrestler telling one of the coaches thanks, but no thanks, he was taking his talent to a bigger, higher-profile school. DeAnna suspected that in many cases the kid was simply mesmerized by the presence of a Division I football team or the recognition that came with attending a school with a household name, even if it happened to be a school whose wrestlers had begun to lose to the guys in the "Boro" singlets on a fairly regular basis. With every snub, DeAnna grew more frustrated. The Scots had downed eastern Pennsylvania power Lehigh 37–14 during the 1986–87 season—"beat the pants off them," DeAnna recalled— yet the following spring a recruit thumbed his nose at coming to Edinboro in favor of Lehigh, because he believed it had a stronger wrestling tradition.

As much as DeAnna adored the kids and as much as he enjoyed the process of turning Edinboro's small Division II program into a player on the Division I scene, in some ways the progress was too deliberate for his tastes. Was it possible that DeAnna had become so programmed by Iowa's success, by the almost instant results, that he was unable to accept the bumps in the road that came with trying to establish something Hawkeye-like in the western Pennsylvania countryside? Was it possible that he had been so conditioned by Gable and the Iowa tradition of excellence that even for all of Edinboro's progress in a short time under his watch he could not accept being anything less than the best? Looking back, DeAnna would agree with that to a point.

"I was proud of what we accomplished, but I never felt like we got where we needed to be," DeAnna said years later. "It took too long. As a wrestler and a coach I never got much satisfaction out of my wins. And the losses—I still can't get them out of my head."

Pam and Mike DeAnna left Edinboro in October of 1990. Mike stunned Jim McDonald by handing him his resignation just weeks before the start of the season, citing personal and professional reasons. "It was like a time bomb dropped on us," McDonald said in a newspaper account of DeAnna's resignation that appeared in the *Erie Times-News*. "It took us totally by surprise."

The DeAnnas packed their belongings and their four kids, including Tony, the seven-year-old blossoming wrestling star, said their goodbyes, and just as they had some six and a half years earlier on that March afternoon after the interview with McDonald, drove away from Edinboro toward an uncertain future. They landed back in Iowa, where DeAnna helped found a youth wrestling club in the town of Ankney. Little Tony DeAnna began to train for a career that would lead him to success in high school in his father's native Cleveland, where the DeAnnas moved after a few years in Ankney, and at Ohio University. Today, Tony DeAnna works for his father in a successful real estate brokerage Mike DeAnna owns not far from his childhood home in the suburbs west of Cleveland.

✦ ✦ ✦ ✦ ✦

Aᴄ̲ᴛᴇʀ DᴇAɴɴᴀ ʟᴇꜰᴛ, Bᴀᴜᴍɢᴀʀᴛɴᴇʀ ʙᴇᴄᴀᴍᴇ ᴛʜᴇ ʟᴏɢɪᴄᴀʟ choice to replace him. He had the credentials and the track record for success as DeAnna's second in command, the man who had, by and large, handled the budget and the recruiting details and a fair share of the fund raising and pubic relations work that had gone into making Edinboro wrestling a recognizable name on the national wrestling scene. It was, by necessity, a quick transition. DeAnna's departure came on the eve of the 1990–91 season, and Baumgartner was too immersed in getting the Scots ready to compete to worry much about the pinch he was in.

"The program was in place," he recalled years later. "Mike and I had worked to get us to the point where we could be competitive, and when Mike left it was my job to keep that going. There wasn't really much time to think about what his leaving meant. Obviously it was going to be tough to replace him, but we didn't have a choice."

Despite that rough 1989 recruiting class, which helped contribute to three straight finishes of twenty-fifth or lower at the nationals, Baumgartner eventually had the Scots back among the nation's elite. He developed some of the talent he had inherited from DeAnna—including Rosselli, who went on to place third and fourth at the nationals—and brought in plenty of his own, including a pair of future NCAA runners-up, Tony Robie and Jason Robison, whose careers helped lay the groundwork for an unprecedented run of success. Baumgartner also brought in as his assistant coach a former All-America lightweight at Penn State with seemingly boundless energy and an untiring work ethic.

Tim Flynn had finished up his master's degree in finance and worked for a while in Hershey, Pennsylvania, selling insurance and hating life. "I was like a lot of people with finance degrees who come out and want to make a million dollars," Flynn recalled. "I

NCAA Division I runners-up Tony Robie (L) and Jason Robison in an undated university publicity photo.

would say that, but I don't think I ever really believed it. I knew I was miserable, and there was a part of me that really missed wrestling. I just knew that when 3:30 in the afternoon rolled around I was supposed to be at practice, and that was missing." By the time he learned through his former coach at Penn State that Edinboro had an opening for an assistant, Flynn had left the insurance gig and taken temporary work managing newspaper routes. He could not have been more ready to take a job, practically any job, that would get him back on the mats. He knew Edinboro had interviewed Zeke Jones, a three-time All-American at Arizona State who was a rising star on the international circuit. He also knew Jones was not exactly begging for the job. For all practical purposes, Flynn was.

The first time Jim McDonald saw Flynn he thought he looked like a pastor. McDonald cannot recall exactly why he sized up Flynn—a man who won 105 matches in college and captained his final Nittany Lions team—and saw someone fit to deliver a Sunday sermon. Maybe it was because, unlike many of the wrestlers McDonald encountered in Edinboro's room—powerfully built and slabbed over with muscle—Flynn seemed slight and thin. Maybe it was because Flynn wasn't particularly loud or boisterous. Maybe it was just McDonald being McDonald. First impressions aside, Flynn got the job.

Flynn would certainly do his share of preaching to Edinboro's wrestlers over the next fifteen years, but when he arrived at Edinboro just before the 1992–93 season it was as Baumgartner's assistant, and as the Olympic hero's new partner charged with helping the Scots continue their ascent among the Division I ranks.

The program grew and flourished under Flynn and Baumgartner. Flynn slid easily into the role of fund-raiser. He was easy to talk to, honest, and straightforward, and his passion for wrestling quickly won over Edinboro's boosters and convinced those close to the program that when it came to understanding the unique set of challenges the Scots faced as an under-funded, under-publicized program competing against the giants in college sports, he got it. Building on an idea DeAnna and Baumgartner had used to some success, Baumgartner and Flynn sold recruits on the notion of coming to Edinboro and becoming a big fish in a small pond.

The two coaches came right out and told kids that, sure, if they picked a Big Ten or Big 12 school, they might enjoy some of the trappings that came with major-college sports in towns with more nightlife or more culture than Edinboro had to offer, but when it came time to make headlines or enjoy campus-wide recognition, there would be no comparison. "We played pretty heavily on that," Baumgartner recalled years later. "Let's face it, if you go to Ohio State to wrestle and Ohio State has a great NCAA tournament, you get some positive ink for a day or two, but as soon as the men's basketball team plays a game—whether it does well or it does poorly—that will overshadow all of the positive wrestling stories you can find. I know that frustrates guys like (University of Minnesota wrestling coach) J Robinson, who has had phenomenal success. They can win a national championship, which they've done, and everybody at the school is more worried about the fact that the new football coach is struggling."

It was that sales pitch that helped Baumgartner land Tony Robie the year before Flynn arrived, which helped land Jason Robison the following year. Inside of a year, the new coaching staff landed two wrestlers whose work ethic and relentless training would become the stuff of legend in Edinboro's practice room and help define the program's next era of greatness. Robie, a craggy, hard-nosed, square-jawed middleweight from inner-city Strong Vincent High School in nearby Erie, had twice finished third in the Pennsylvania state high school tournament, but Baumgartner saw in him potential that had barely been tapped when he got to Edinboro in the fall of 1992. Robison followed the next season, a PIAA champion from Allison Park, outside Pittsburgh, who away from the mat wore glasses that made him look a little like an Algebra teacher and who had been so intrigued by the notion of wrestling under Baumgartner that Edinboro was the only school he seriously considered.

The afternoon of his first official college practice, Robie walked into a wrestling room he described as very much in transition. There was undeniable talent, including Rosselli, who was winding down a brilliant, 136-win career; Tom Shifflet, who would become a three-time All-American; and a few somewhat lesser-known names such as Ken Bauer, a workhorse who won 94 career matches without reaching the NCAA medal stand.

There was also what Robie described as a handful of wrestlers who were simply hanging on, providing little in the way of competition or motivation and who, through their actions and, in some cases, inaction, generally served as distractions to those wrestlers who were training seriously to become national champions. Part of the reason was that Baumgartner had been traveling heavily for international competitions in preparation for the 1992 Olympic Games, and before Flynn's arrival he had been forced to get by with more volunteer assistant coaching help than usual thanks to a budget crunch brought on by statewide educational cutbacks. Flynn called the atmosphere when he arrived "generally negative" and recalls several times when he questioned whether he would even want to stay beyond that first, difficult 1992–93 season.

After Edinboro lost at West Virginia, 21–14, late in a season that would end with a 6–7 dual-meet record and a sixth-place finish in the Eastern Wrestling League, Flynn stormed off the floor of the West Virginia University Coliseum in Morgantown and slammed his fist against the wall in what he described years later as an angry, tearful outburst. "I came from Penn State and our mindset was, you womp West Virginia, and here we were losing to them," Flynn recalled. "We just never sucked that bad at Penn State, and I remember thinking that we legitimately sucked. We had Lou and we had Shifflet, but really not much else. I thought, things are going to change or Timmy's not gonna be around much longer." The Scots did manage a fifteenth-place finish at that year's NCAA tournament, but that was on the strength of top-six finishes by Rosselli and Shifflet, two of the few wrestlers who, in Flynn's mind, didn't suck.

"It wasn't good," Robie recalled years later of the overall atmosphere in the practice room during his first winter at Edinboro. "You had guys who were there to work, and you had guys who seemed like they were there to do just about everything but work. It took a little time, but we weeded them out and we got a great bunch of guys in the room."

Robie's emergence as a leader and Robison's arrival the following spring provided a huge lift. Robison was cut of the same cloth as Robie, a relentless trainer who tolerated zero shenanigans. The two, along with Shifflet, quickly took roles front and center in Edinboro's room after Rosselli finished up in 1993 and began to train for international competition while staying on as a volunteer assistant.

With Shifflet, Robie, and Robison leading no-nonsense practices, Flynn practically bouncing off the walls and preaching to them to share his through-the-roof expectations, and Baumgartner on a more regular, post-Olympics schedule, the improvement was rapid and dramatic.

Robison's arrival was followed by three other significant

recruits with sparkling high school credentials—Marco Sanchez, Kevin Saniga, and Matt Stein, the latter two making significant contributions over the next five years. While the Scots failed to produce an All-American during the 1993–94 season, they were rounding into a solid team. They went 15–2 in dual meets, setting the stage for a run that would produce the program's best finish ever at the nationals.

"Once we got Robison and Saniga it was like, bam, the recruits just started rolling in. Really good kids. I remember being out there on the road and people saying, 'Damn, you got this guy, too?'" Flynn recalls. "It was nice. But Bruce and I worked hard to get those guys."

Those early Baumgartner-Flynn recruiting classes culminated in 1996–97, when Edinboro went 14–0 in dual meets—including a 27–13 spanking of West Virginia and wins over Ohio State, Pittsburgh, Arizona State, and Oregon State—and finished sixth at the nationals, the highest NCAA Division I showing in the program's history. Shifflet was third that year, while Robie and Robison, who had begun to come into their own, finished fifth and seventh, respectively. That year's nationals, in the shadow of Gable's great Hawkeyes program in Cedar Falls, Iowa, would be the last for Baumgartner and Flynn together, though. After the season, Baumgartner, who was preparing to make one last run at an Olympic gold medal in 1996, became Edinboro's athletic director. Jim McDonald, whose temper and persistence had helped elevate the program to the Division I level twelve years earlier, retired to pursue overseas missionary work, in which he remains deeply involved. Flynn, the bundle of energy who had inexplicably struck McDonald as a preacher five years earlier, would take his place, and Lou Rosselli would be his assistant.

Looking back on the program's first twelve years at the Division I level, McDonald said he left with a good feeling.

"During my thirty-two years at Edinboro, I had always told our coaches that there was no reason they couldn't be successful at the national level," McDonald said twelve years after leaving Edinboro. "Sometimes that was probably stupidity or pride on my part, but I truly believed it. And I believed it when I told Mike

Edinboro coaches Tim Flynn (L) and Bruce Baumgartner (C) with trainer
Gary Hanna (R) during a 1997 home dual meet.

DeAnna and Bruce Baumgartner. I was pretty bent on the fact
that we were going to succeed, and we did."

McDonald's retirement and Baumgartner's resignation
represented yet another massive transition, but one eased by
the building blocks already in place. Baumgartner would still
be around, his presence felt not only as a recruiting aid but as a
resource to the young coaches. The atmosphere in the practice
room had long since been established and cultivated. O'Day
recalled later that the early years established a tenacious sense of
competition at practices and even during conditioning workouts.
Every running session became a race, and wrestlers would push
one another into ditches in an attempt to win. In subsequent
years, Robie, Robison and Koscheck helped add the toughness
and attitude. Even with DeAnna and McDonald gone and
Baumgartner stepping aside, the recipe remained for Flynn and
Rosselli to brew up another national champion. All they needed
were the right ingredients.

| Chapter Nine |

Koscheck

S EAN O'DAY'S FINESSE AND EXPLOSIVENESS ENABLED HIM TO deliver the program's first NCAA Division I championship, but under Baumgartner and later Flynn, this next wave of great Edinboro wrestlers would be fronted by brutishly strong, physically dominating bullies like Tony Robie and Jason Robison. While DeAnna and Baumgartner carefully picked their spots for O'Day to go hard in live action during practices, the coaches simply turned Robie and Robison loose on each other and on anyone else who happened to be nearby and let them whale away. "The tide started to turn with Robie," Flynn later recalled. "He provided fight in the room. Robie was just this tough kid from Erie, and some of the guys on the team weren't one-tenth as tough." Robie and Robison didn't just beat opponents, they broke them mentally, and sometimes physically. Their styles were established long before they got to Edinboro, but their time in the college wrestling room, when they were able to feed off of one another's intensity every day, made them meaner and even more unflinching in their willingness to go hard all the time. And that rubbed off on the other wrestlers.

"Tony needed the battle," Baumgartner recalled of Robie. "If he came out of the practice room and didn't spend at least an hour pounding on somebody he didn't feel like he'd gotten anything done."

Robie capped a 126-win career with a runner-up finish at the 1997 nationals, losing to Iowa's Joe Williams. Robison placed second the following year after taking a 45–0 record and a No. 1 national ranking into the title bout, where he lost 6–4 in overtime

Josh Koscheck in an undated university publicity photo. Koscheck would become Edinboro's second NCAAA Division I champ.

to Minnesota's Tim Hartung. He graduated as the school's all-time wins leader, with 145 career victories. Along with Robie, Robison shared the distinction of helping to shape Edinboro's profile as a place where blue-chip recruits—and even those who weren't quite as sought after—could find coaches capable of fully developing their talent and helping them bloom into national title contenders. Years later, Robison credited Flynn for much of his success. What Flynn lacked in stature he made up for in drive, and Robison recalls one of the turning points in his career coming as the result of a classic Flynn tactic. Robison, a freshman, had just gone 1–2 in his first trip to the nationals in 1994. The tournament was held at the University of North Carolina that year, and the morning after the finals, Flynn rousted Robison from his hotel bed at dawn and ordered the dejected young wrestler to join him for a long run through the streets of Chapel Hill. Flynn's message was clear—last season might have been barely twelve hours old, but it was over. It was time to move forward and get better. Robison received it loud and clear.

DeAnna, Baumgartner, and Flynn all believed they could take a wrestler of modest athletic ability and, with the right work ethic and attitude, make him great, regardless of how he fared before he stepped through the doorway into Edinboro's practice room. That theory was put to the test in the winter of 1997–98 with an enigmatic young recruit from the southwestern Pennsylvania foothills who might ultimately have done more to raise Edinboro's wrestling profile than anyone other than Bruce Baumgartner.

⊕   ⊕   ⊕   ⊕   ⊕

IN MARCH 1997, FLYNN AND ASSISTANT COACH GARY ASTORINO, Edinboro's recruiting coordinator, had been pursuing Vince DeAugustine, a wrestler from Hempfield, Pennsylvania, outside Pittsburgh, when they discovered Josh Koscheck. DeAugustine was seeking a second straight PIAA Class AAA title that season, and Koscheck was his opponent in the state final at 160 pounds. DeAugustine won the match, 2–1, but it was Koscheck who intrigued Flynn and Astorino, and they reported back to Baumgartner that this kid was the quintessential diamond in the rough.

Koscheck grew up in Waynesburg, an old coal town near the Pennsylvania–West Virginia line. He never knew his father, and his teenage mother had given him up to her parents to raise. By the time he was a senior in high school, Koscheck was a physical specimen with tremendous athletic ability and no clear idea of what to do next. Pitt had shown some interest in him for wrestling, and a handful of Division II and III football schools were recruiting him as a defensive back. Koscheck loved to play football, and he had a serious girlfriend at the time, so wrestling at Pitt or playing football at a local college would keep him close to home. But after the state wrestling tournament, when he seemingly came from nowhere as someone who had never contended for a medal before to post a runner-up finish, suddenly his options multiplied.

Flynn recalls watching Koscheck in an all-star match a week after the PIAA tournament. Koscheck was wrestling a kid from Wisconsin in a dual meet that was part of the run-up to the main event, Pittsburgh's Dapper Dan Classic, one of the nation's oldest all-star wrestling events.

"He was just really, really rugged," Flynn recalled. "He was out there slugging some kid from Wisconsin, and he was being pretty rough. I remember talking to him afterward and telling him. 'I don't know how good a football player you are, but you're going to be something in wrestling.'"

Until then, Koscheck had been leaning toward football, but something at the tail end of his senior wrestling season changed things. Koscheck had been cutting more than 30 pounds to get to 130 or 135 his first three years in high school and not having much success. But his senior year he decided to bulk up to 160 to get ready for college football, and suddenly he was winning on the mat. When he reached the state final and lost, he had enough of a taste of the sport to realize he wanted more.

"I felt like I had unfinished business in wrestling," Koscheck recalled ten years later. "I never liked the whole aspect of team. I've always been into the individual part of it. Some people might say that's selfish. Hey, call me selfish."

It didn't hurt that Koscheck loved to fly fish, and Lake Erie's tributary streams offered some of the best steelhead trout fishing in the world. So by the spring of 1997, Koscheck was ready to sign on with Baumgartner and Flynn. The steelhead and his competitive streak had gotten him to Edinboro. As it turned out, keeping him there would not be easy.

Koscheck bought into Flynn's pitch, although with his academic record he was a non-qualifier, forced to sit out his first season as a redshirt until he established his grades in college. That was tougher than Koscheck imagined. Getting out of bed for 6 a.m. workouts and training harder than he ever had in his life—without the opportunity to compete for a varsity spot—made college life a grind. He warmed slowly to school, slower still to Baumgartner's and Flynn's demands.

"I hated it," Koscheck recalled. "My priorities weren't right. I had pretty much raised myself and done my own thing. I mean, my grandparents were there, but they were my grandparents and there was a generation gap. They told me to make my own way, and I just took care of myself. I guess the biggest thing when I got to Edinboro was I was never used to somebody telling me what to do. That was the hard part."

Flynn remembers Koscheck simply being lazy. He had considerable athletic talent and was certainly hard-nosed enough to compete in Edinboro's practice room, but for at least the first half of his freshman season he refused to give himself over to a proven system that had made stars of wrestlers like O'Day, Robie, and Robison. The coaches were out of ideas for how to motivate him. They finally decided that if Koscheck was going to come around, he would have to come around on his own terms.

For reasons that even Koscheck can't fully explain, he returned to campus right after Christmas break, entered the practice room and began to unleash Holy Hell. He sidled up to Robie and Robison, allowed Rosselli to take him under his wing, and bought into the training and the early workouts and the going to class. That spring he accompanied Robie and Rosselli to the U.S. Open, a precursor to some of the top international events, and won four matches. It was unusual for a true freshman to go to the Open and win, much less win four times. Koscheck said the tournament was an eye-opener for him. He returned believing he could have success, believing he belonged in Division I wrestling, believing he belonged at Edinboro. "I've never seen a quicker turnaround," Flynn recalled. "One day he just decided, that's it, I'm f---king going to win." Koscheck stayed in Edinboro the following summer and trained. When practices resumed in the fall, it was clear he had bought into the system lock, stock, and barrel. Baumgartner was athletic director, and Flynn replaced him as head coach, with Rosselli moving up to full-time assistant. Robie had graduated but remained as an assistant, but Robison was gone. Senior Mark Samples capped his career with an All-America finish at the 1999 nationals, but there was a leadership void in the room, and Koscheck, as a redshirt freshman, stepped headlong into it.

"All of a sudden we had this vocal hard ass who didn't put up with s--t," Flynn recalled. "We had a coach that wasn't on staff; he was on the team. He would be out and see a freshman trying to drink and drive and grab his keys and—ka-plow!—you ain't drivin'."

"He was kind of a loner. He didn't care if people liked him. Even after he won the NCAAs, we would be moving mats for a match and he would grab the mat and say, 'Come on you f--kers, let's go!' He wasn't the national champ who said, 'I shouldn't have to move mats.' He was the national champ who said, 'Let's get this done, or someone gets punched in the mouth.'"

Just as importantly, Koscheck backed it up on the mat during his redshirt freshman season. He went to the prestigious Las Vegas Invitational and knocked off second-ranked Sam Kline of West Virginia en route to a runner-up finish. At the nationals that year in Penn State, Koscheck went in seeded tenth, lost in the quarterfinals, but rebounded to win five straight consolation matches before settling for fourth. It was there at State College that Koscheck experienced an epiphany. Following Koscheck's 6–4 loss to Wisconsin's seventh-seeded Kole Clausen in the quarters, Flynn pulled him into a concourse off the arena floor and challenged his manhood. By that time, Flynn understood how Koscheck was wired. In Koscheck's mind, anyone he beat, he beat because he was tougher than they were. Anyone he lost to, he lost to because, in his words, he "wrestled like a pussy." There was no middle ground. Koscheck was unwilling to ever concede that a wrestler was better or stronger than he was. That would be admitting something he wasn't prepared to deal with. So Flynn backed Koscheck against a wall, put a finger in his face and asked, in an even tone, "You know why you lost? Because you were a pussy out there." Koscheck nodded his head. Flynn was right. Koscheck would make sure it never happened again.

There would be more gut-checks for Koscheck, though, and the next one came almost exactly one year later in the national finals against a top-seeded senior from Oklahoma named Byron Tucker. Koscheck, a third-year sophomore, had gone into the tournament seeded third. He knocked off second-seeded Rick

Springman of Penn to reach the final, but that's where his mind began playing tricks on him. Koscheck began buying into his own doubts, that Tucker was older, that he had been to the finals before, that, just maybe, Koscheck was ahead of schedule and really wasn't ready to wrestle for a national title against such a seasoned opponent. The result was a 3–0 loss in which Koscheck wasn't able to muster anything. His balls-out, physical, wide-open style seemed powerless against the steady, rock-solid Tucker. His game plan would not work. "I didn't believe I could beat him," Koscheck said years later. "In a way, I was just happy to be there. Realistically I never thought I could be national champion. I believed I could be an All-American. After that, I changed my mind."

As he had the previous two summers, Koscheck stayed in Edinboro and trained. He trained harder than he had the year before, running more, lifting more, drilling more. He became even tougher on his teammates in the practice room, and at one point Flynn and Rosselli returned from a recruiting trip to find a handful of wrestlers in their office begging them to remind Koscheck that he wasn't really the coach. But Koscheck couldn't see it any other way. He knew what his goals were and he didn't think anyone else in the room should be aiming any lower than he was. To his way of thinking, Edinboro's wrestling program was only as strong as its weakest link, and Koscheck made it his mission to seek out that link and strengthen it—or at least call it a pussy. "You have to be selfish to be a champion," Koscheck said years later, a statement that seemed to contradict how hard he rode his teammates in the room. But even while he was losing himself in his own training, he was pushing them to match his intensity. Many years later, Koscheck remarked that "there were plenty of guys who came through Edinboro's room who should have been national champs, but they just didn't apply themselves the way I did, or the way Gregor Gillespie or Sean O'Day did."

That season, as a junior, Koscheck applied himself like no other wrestler in the program's history. He went 42–0, and most of his matches weren't close. He was taken down once all season, early on at the NWCA National Duals, and after that he stepped up his training further and simply blitzed the 174-pound weight class at the nationals, winning his five matches by a combined score of 41–7, including an 8–1 win over Army's third-seeded Maurice Worthy in the final. The win came in Iowa City, home of Gable's Hawkeyes and DeAnna's college stomping grounds. Like Gable and DeAnna, Koscheck had a hard time savoring the title. He posted Edinboro's first undefeated Division I season, becoming a kid who never placed at the state tournament until his senior year, who nearly quit school out of homesickness and laziness, and conquered the college wrestling world. But there was more work to be done.

⊕ ⊕ ⊕ ⊕ ⊕

FLYNN EXPLAINED YEARS LATER THAT KOSCHECK'S INFLUENCE ON Edinboro's wrestling program actually extended long past his time on campus. The same could be said for O'Day, Robie, or Robison. Obviously for the four or five years they were at Edinboro their work ethic and success rubbed off on teammates. But Flynn believed that in Koscheck's case in particular, the freshmen who watched him train and compete during his senior season carried that image with them and shared it with future recruits, making it possible for Koscheck to impact dozens of wrestlers, some of whom he never even met. "One Josh Koscheck could affect your program for ten years," Flynn said. "There was no substitute for that." The reason Flynn believed so strongly in Koscheck's influence is, in large part, because of a weightlifting mishap that occurred over the summer between Koscheck's junior and senior years, an injury that would not heal until he underwent surgery weeks after the 2002 nationals in Albany, New York, an injury that set a new standard for toughness in Edinboro's room.

Koscheck had been working out in the weight room in the basement of McComb Fieldhouse when he ruptured a disc in his neck. He thought it was a muscle pull, something that would resolve itself with rest and a little Icy Hot, but as the season approached it became obvious it was not going away. The pain was numbing, and with his title defense at hand Koscheck found himself unable to work out, unable to lift, unable to perform

Josh Koscheck checks the time remaining in his 8-1 win over Army's Maurice Worthy in the 2001 NCAA 174-pound final at Iowa City, Iowa.

almost any wrestling activity except riding a stationary bike while his teammates ground one another into dust in the practice room. It was no way to start out a season in which Koscheck, riding a forty-two-match winning streak, was trying to become the first two-time national champ in school history. But he had no choice. His red shirt was used up, and odds were the NCAA would not grant him a sixth year through a medical hardship exemption. He had to compete, but he would be miserable.

No matter what Koscheck and Edinboro's training staff did, there was no lasting relief. Flynn and Koscheck downplayed the injury for fear opponents would pick up on its severity and spend an entire seven-minute match trying to beat Koscheck into submission. Wrestling was that type of sport. A weakness or an injury was something to be attacked, exploited, capitalized on. If there was no valor in sitting out with anything less than debilitating pain, there was no valor in avoiding the body part that was hurting on a guy who was tough enough to wrestle in spite of it.

Early in the season, at the National Wrestling Coaches Association (NWCA) National Duals in Columbus, Ohio, in December 2001, there were startling signs that Koscheck might not be himself. He lost at the duals to Otto Olson of Michigan, a tough, highly ranked wrestler, but an opponent Koscheck would almost certainly handle if he were 100 percent. "He looked bad," Flynn recalled. "He got so tired because he couldn't train. You can ride the bike all you want, but you don't have that muscle endurance. He would be at practice but he couldn't practice. He was frustrated, and it was tough for us to watch." Later in the season, a skin infection forced Koscheck to sit out a dual meet against West Virginia, denying him the chance to match up against the Mountaineers' redshirt freshman sensation, Greg Jones. The rumbles began that Koscheck might have been hurt worse than anyone thought and that he was ducking Jones to avoid exposing the injury's severity. By the time the postseason rolled around, Koscheck had no choice but to go out and struggle through matches as best he could. His pursuit of a third straight Eastern Wrestling League (EWL) championship ended with a loss to Jones in the final and meant he would enter the nationals as the No. 3 seed, behind Jones and Olson. He still had a chance to repeat his championship, but the road would be tougher.

Koscheck won his first two matches at that year's nationals at Pepsi Arena in Albany, where most of the attention swirled around Iowa State senior 197-pounder Cael Sanderson's pursuit of perfection. Sanderson was in the process of winning his fourth national title without losing a single match, and ESPN, CNN, *Sports Illustrated,* and virtually every other national media outlet was there to document every move he made. With all the fuss over Sanderson, it was easy to miss the compelling story unfolding in the 174-pound bracket.

The wins put Koscheck on course for a rematch with Jones in the national semifinals, but first he would have to beat Penn's sixth-seeded Rick Springman, whom he had upset two years earlier to reach his first final. Perhaps because of the toll the postseason had taken, or the pressure Springman applied throughout the match, Koscheck faltered badly, losing 6–0 to drop into the consolations, a devastating blow for a healthy wrestler, much less for a wrestler whose throbbing neck could knock him out of the tournament at any time. By then it was Friday afternoon, and Koscheck had to win one more match that evening to become Edinboro's first four-time All-American. He retreated to the bowels of Pepsi Arena to receive treatment on his neck, rested for a couple of hours, then came back and ground out a 4–0 win over Drexel's Ben Chunko to clinch a medal. The look on his face after the match was more relief than elation, and Koscheck went back to his room at the team hotel and collapsed.

When Flynn went to get him in the morning, the coach was stunned by what he saw. Koscheck was groggy and could barely hold up his head. The pain made him wince when he talked. Flynn tried to convince him to forfeit his next two matches and settle for eighth place, if only because he wasn't sure he could watch him torture himself any further. "He was a mess," Flynn recalled. "I actually said, 'You don't have to wrestle.'"

Ignoring his coach, Koscheck asked what place Edinboro was in and how high it could finish in the team race.

"Don't do it for me, bud," Flynn replied. "My job is secure. Edinboro will be all right."

"I'm wrestling," Koscheck insisted.

"He was wrestling for the team," Flynn recalled. "He didn't say, 'I want to get third,' he said, 'How high can we go?'"

Koscheck went back out that morning and, in a courageous effort whose full magnitude escaped most everyone watching in the arena, dispatched Air Force's Terry Parham to ensure himself a top-five finish, then beat the top-seeded Olson, who had been upset in the semifinals, to reach the third-place match. His last collegiate bout looked like vintage Koscheck. He dominated Oregon State's Nathan Coy 9–1, not just winning, but posting a major decision that earned Edinboro a bonus in the team race. The Scots finished fourteenth, and junior Cory Ace joined Koscheck as an All-American with an eighth-place finish.

A few weeks later, Koscheck underwent surgery to repair the

bulging disc in his neck. Afterward, his doctor told him the injury was so severe that 99 percent of people who had it would have been unable to get out of bed and brush their teeth in the morning, much less compete at a high level against elite college wrestlers. "Here's a guy that couldn't move his dang neck, couldn't work out all season, and he took third in the country," Flynn recalled years later. "That was impressive."

That was Koscheck. It should come as no surprise that Koscheck, who never liked to be told what to do, went his own way after college. Instead of training for the Olympics, as everyone expected him to do, he became fascinated with mixed martial arts (MMA), which combines elements of wrestling, boxing, and jujitsu, and became one of the stars of a reality show, "The Ultimate Fighter," that launched him into a new career. By early 2008, he was one of the top welterweight contenders in the Ultimate Fighting Championships, the fastest growing of the MMA organizations.

In November 2007, about five years after his last college wrestling match, Koscheck returned to Edinboro to help with a coaching clinic and to train with Flynn and his wrestlers for a few days. Sitting on a couch in the wrestling suite, Koscheck talked about the money and the lifestyle that MMA had helped him achieve. He had met movie stars and toured with musicians, even landing a bit in a music video. But coming back to McComb made him sentimental. He recalled Robie telling him, while he was down in the dumps during his true freshman year, to stick it out because everything he would ever do in life after wrestling would be easy. He insisted that Edinboro's practice room "is one of the best rooms in the country. It doesn't get all the glory. It doesn't get all the media attention. But the way it produces great wrestlers is insane."

Mostly he thanked Baumgartner and Flynn, over and over, for giving him the chance to succeed, particularly Flynn, whom he had teased after winning his national title by insisting that one of the hallways in the new house Flynn bought that year along the fairway of a golf course just outside Edinboro should be named "The Koscheck Wing."

Actually, Koscheck, who went from an unknown non-qualifier to an NCAA champion and Academic All-American by the end of his college career, felt he owed the coach more than he could possibly repay.

"The thing about Flynn," Koscheck recalled, "he believed in me more than I believed in myself. When you find someone like that, you'll do anything for that person."

Josh Koscheck atop the medal stand after winning the 174-pound national championship at the 2001 NCAA tournament at Carver-Hawkeye Arena in Iowa City, Iowa.

| Chapter Ten |

Gillespie

IN ALMOST ANY CONVERSATION ABOUT COLLEGE WRESTLING, OR wrestling at any level for that matter, someone will probably mention the word *room*, often in relation to a certain university or coach. You might hear a reference to "Gable's room," or a reference to "Oklahoma State's room," or perhaps a reference to someone's "high school room." In most cases—assuming it's not a conversation among carpenters—they're not talking about the two-by-fours and drywall and the mats and the lights and the temperature control system—the things that form the structure in which a wrestling team drills and trains. They're talking about the metaphysical room, which is to say that "Gable's room" wasn't just a sweaty place with four walls, it was the embodiment of Gable's coaching philosophy. To be trained in "Gable's room" meant having soaked up the legendary coach's teaching and survived his brutal drill sessions and conditioning regimen. It meant having been ingrained with the Iowa tradition, to have trained on the same mats, in the same space, and beneath the weight of the same expectations that had been placed on the great Hawkeye stars of the past.

By the fall of 2005, the basement of McComb Fieldhouse had been home to "DeAnna's room," "Baumgartner's room," and finally "Flynn's room." But in a larger, more general sense, it was "Edinboro's room," and that reference embodied the attitude that had grown from those early days when DeAnna and Baumgartner and Hahesy and Furey had helped cut a patch for the small school on the college wrestling landscape. Any reference to a wrestler who had come from "Edinboro's room" carried

Gregor Gillespie reacts after a win over Minnesota's Dustin Schlatter in the 2007 NCAA Semifinals at the Palace of Auburn Hills.

with it the implication of having learned to do more with less. It meant having bucked the odds that suggested an under-funded Division II school far removed from the sport's breadbasket could thrive and knock heads with the powers from the Big Ten and Big 12. It meant training in a weight room that looked more like a dungeon. It meant showing up at fund-raisers so the team could fly to Las Vegas for a wrestling tournament instead of busing to one closer to home. It meant competing in front of home crowds that numbered in the hundreds instead of the thousands who routinely showed up to watch Penn State, Iowa, Oklahoma State, and Minnesota.

Edinboro's best wrestlers talked about their room with reverence, wore it as a badge of honor. Deonte Penn, a two-time All-American from Cleveland who won 114 matches from 2002 to 2007, said he took more satisfaction beating opponents from Michigan, Ohio State, or Nebraska knowing that they had been groomed in shiny, high-tech facilities. Meanwhile, he and his teammates flipped a tractor tire end-for-end across the mats in Edinboro's room as part of a diabolical preseason conditioning program, of which Rosselli would later say with no small amount of pride: "When you go through one of my workouts you're not saying, 'Oh my God, I'm tired.' You're saying, 'Oh my God, I think I'm going to f—king die.' It's like I'm sticking a knife right into your heart."

When Koscheck returned to Edinboro to train in the fall of 2007, he toured the new weight room and cardio center the school had built in the basement of McComb to replace the one that had been there, virtually untouched, since DeAnna and Baumgartner arrived twenty-three years earlier. Koscheck knew the school needed new equipment, but the thought of something so modern and clean almost repulsed him.

"Bruce Baumgartner won the Olympics in that old s--tty weight room, and it was good enough for him," Koscheck said. "It's not about how pretty your stuff is. It's not about how much money you have. It's all about dedication and who you surround yourself with. The facilities here when I was here were garbage. The practice room was crap. But it didn't matter. We won."

Edinboro's crappy little room was chugging along when Gregor Gillespie arrived late in the summer of 2005. Koscheck had been gone for almost four years, but wrestlers like Matt King—a two-time All-American who placed fourth in 2003 and third in 2004—and Shawn Bunch—a finalist in 2005—had replaced him and kept Edinboro in the national consciousness, even though the Scots had slid out of the top twenty at the nationals three straight years.

Gillespie was not the most celebrated member of the 2005 recruiting class. That distinction probably went to Pat Bradshaw, a 197-pound PIAA champion from nearby Saegertown who was being counted on to become the first local kid since Tony Robie in the mid-1990s to earn All-America honors at Edinboro. Bradshaw was joined by heavyweight Terry Tate from Tyrone, Pennsylvania, another state champion. To many of the program's observers, the incoming class that year consisted primarily of Bradshaw and Tate, two Pennsylvania-bred stars with high upsides, and this kid with the curious-sounding name from a part of New York state that was not known for producing top-notch college wrestling talent.

In other words, Gillespie was just the sort of unknown, untapped prospect that had come to signify almost any reference to "Edinboro's room."

✦   ✦   ✦   ✦   ✦

B RAD GILLESPIE WRESTLED IN COLLEGE AND PASSED HIS LOVE FOR the sport along to his sons, Gregor and Torsten. In the basement of their home in Webster, New York, outside Rochester, Brad fashioned a wrestling room with parts of mats stretched across the floor and pushed up the walls, and his two sons scrapped and rolled and whaled on one another while he taught them some basic technique. It became clear fairly early on that Gregor, like Brad, would have a wrestler's small frame. Gregor was quick, which helped him excel at soccer, but his mother, Susan, steered him away from football for fear he would get hurt. Gregor dabbled in other sports but found his passion on the mats, and by the time he reached seventh grade he was good enough to beat most of the varsity wrestlers in his part of the state. In New York, eighth graders are allowed to compete in wrestling at the high school level, and the state's athletic association also makes a provision for seventh graders to do so if they can pass a standards test of physical ability. Gillespie attempted to pass the test but, at barely five feet tall, couldn't broad jump the seven and a half feet the standards test required. That meant he was relegated to junior varsity, and he opened the season by pinning his first thirty opponents. By December it became obvious he was too good for jayvees, and an exception was made to allow him to compete for the varsity team at Webster Schroeder, the local high school. Standards test be damned, Gillespie qualified for the New York state championships that year. He didn't place, but it was the last time he wouldn't.

From his eighth-grade season through his senior year, Gillespie won 238 matches and lost only 14. He earned five state medals, including a pair of titles, and never finished lower than third. Yet he was still virtually ignored by all of the big wrestling powers, with offers only from a few Mid-American Conference schools, including Buffalo. It seemed that no one was sold on a kid from outside of New York's wrestling hotbeds of Long Island and the Buffalo area, a kid who was a terror from the top position and relied heavily on tilts and cradles—moves that were tough to use consistently against top Division I opponents.

Even a fourth-place finish at the Junior Nationals in 2004 failed to attract much attention from the heavyweights, and Gillespie found himself winding down his high school career without the sort of offers a wrestler with his resume might expect. Part of it had to do with his weight class on the national scene. The 145-pound class was top-heavy in 2005, led by intensely recruited blue-chip prospects Dustin Schlatter from Ohio, who would wind up at Minnesota, and Brent Metcalf from Michigan, who signed with Virginia Tech and later transferred to Iowa.

On a lark two years earlier, Gillespie had unwittingly attracted Flynn's attention. It was a silly thing, really. Gillespie had been preparing to wrestle in the New York state finals as a sophomore when someone handed him a questionnaire to fill out so the television announcers could read off insightful-sounding tidbits while he rolled around on the mat. One question asked which colleges he was considering. Gillespie was still so young that college was barely on his radar screen. Stuck for a school, he leaned over and peaked at the questionnaire another New York

Edinboro Olympians Lou Rosselli (L) and Bruce Baumgartner (R) in a
1996 university publicity photo.

wrestler, senior Nate Mumbulo, was filling out. Under "colleges
considering," Mumbulo had written "Edinboro."

Gillespie did the same.

A few weeks later Gillespie received a call from Flynn, who
had borrowed a tape of the telecast of the New York finals from
another coach and heard the announcer read off Gillespie's
college interest.

Edinboro NCAA All-American and 1996 Olympian Lou Rosselli in an undated training photo taken in Edinboro's wrestling room.

"Uh, I just wrote something down," Gillespie confessed to Flynn. "I wasn't sure what to put."

Two years later, after Flynn and Rosselli had visited his home and Gillespie had taken only his second official visit to check out a campus—the other was to UNC–Greensboro—Gregor and Brad Gillespie sat at one of Edinboro's two traffic lights—the one at the center of the little college town, at the intersection with three gas stations and the Crossroads Dinor—and waited for the signal to turn green. "This is where I want to go, Dad," Gregor told Brad. "This is the place."

✛   ✛   ✛   ✛   ✛

GILLESPIE'S ARRIVAL CAME AT WHAT TURNED OUT TO BE A CRUCIAL time. The program was in need of new stars. No one knew it then, but Rosselli would be gone inside of ten months for Ohio State, leaving a huge void. Bunch, the lightning-quick Kansan who had transformed himself from an outrageously talented prospect with questionable work habits to one of the program's great success stories, would be gone, too, leaving as a two-time All-American and Edinboro's first national finalist since Koscheck.

Fortunately, Gillespie was able to spend a full season with Rosselli and Bunch before they left, and the experience was priceless. Rosselli handled a lot of Edinboro's conditioning, the sessions that had helped Bunch turn the corner from high school prospect to elite college talent.

The sessions could be downright evil. Flynn and Rosselli filled five-gallon buckets with concrete and made the wrestlers run with one in each hand. They filled wheelbarrows with forty-five-pound weight plates and made them push them around campus. Then they dumped the weights, put a teammate in the wheelbarrow, and made them push them up hills. Then there was the tractor tire. And the drilling. And the five- and six-mile runs.

All of it was designed to prove one thing. These kids might have thought they showed up to college ready to wrestle in college, but they had no idea how wrong they were. Rosselli recalled:

The hardest thing for these guys is learning how hard they have to work at this level. The guys who were elite guys in high school, they didn't have to work. They basically kicked the s--t out of people until March, then they got some tough matches. When they get here, they have to work like they never had to work, because they can't get by on talent alone anymore.

You look at Shawn Bunch, and when he got here he had no idea how to work, because he always got by on his talent. His first year he would have a great practice, then a decent one, then a s---ty one, then a great one, then another s---ty one. So basically he was only practicing twice a week, because that's all he was getting out of it. That won't cut it at this level. If you want to be good at this level, you have to have a great practice every day, because that's what the guys at Iowa and Oklahoma State and Minnesota are doing.

Gillespie soaked all of that in, and he got off to a hot start, the hottest by far by any Edinboro true freshman. He won his first twenty-three matches before losing twice at the Southern Scuffle in Greensboro, North Carolina, in December. He entered the nationals with a 15–2 record against NCAA qualifiers, and he reached the quarterfinals before losing 5–3 to second-seeded Ty Eustice of Iowa. Gillespie lost one more time before ending the tournament with a win in the seventh-place match. He had gone 40–4 as a true freshman, and he'd proven that the kid from the soft part of New York state could win big in Division I wrestling, and he could do it with a college-honed variation of his style.

In high school, Gillespie had been one of those wrestlers Rosselli talked about, who had gotten by most of the time on pure talent. He was always in shape, always overflowing with energy. That was just his personality. Even Brad had called him a "type-A, hyper-intense kid." Gregor never caused much trouble, but he also didn't require much sleep. At one point his parents imposed a curfew and were impressed to see him consistently arriving home ten minutes early, only to find out later that he would retreat to his room, wait for the coast to clear, and sneak out the window to meet his buddies around back. "Once he makes his mind up he's going to do something," Brad said, "well, good luck trying to stop him."

That was precisely Gregor's mindset one year later, when

he was back at the nationals as a sophomore, this time as the fifth seed and as a long shot to win. As a freshman, he started the year using the same stuff he relied on as a high school star. Get a quick takedown and go to work tilting his opponent, often ending matches in the first or second period with technical falls. But eventually the scouting report on Gillespie took shape, and opponents were stopping his tilts and fighting off his cradles. The first signs of the scouting reports emerged at the Southern Scuffle, where he was finding it difficult to score.

So he made up his mind he would become even better on his feet and learn to grind out wins with strategy instead of an onslaught of points from the top position. That helped carry him to the nationals, and it got him back there his sophomore year, to the Palace of Auburn Hills, in March 2007.

By the time he reached his second NCAA tournament, Gillespie had become well-rounded enough to win any kind of match an opponent wanted to wrestle.

Good luck trying to stop him.

His first match was a 9–5 win over Sam Alvarenga of Virginia Military Institute, the only unseeded wrestler he would face in the 149-pound bracket. After the first win, Gillespie gained steam, posting an 11–2 major decision over Penn State's twelfth-seeded Dan Vallimont. Gillespie was now in the quarterfinals against Cornell's fourth-seeded Jordan Leen, who had handed him one of his two losses during the regular season. Gillespie won 6–2.

Next up: Schlatter, the top seed, the wrestler who had overshadowed Gillespie in their recruiting class by landing at Minnesota, and then overshadowed him again by winning the nationals as a true freshman. Schlatter had reached the semifinals with that sixty-five-match winning streak, the longest in the nation. The crowd of more than 15,000 was abuzz during the match, but not because of Gillespie or Schlatter, who was the heavy favorite. Instead, the fuss was over third-seeded local star Josh Churella, who on the adjacent mat was moving one step closer to a Cinderella finish in the national tournament by downing Ohio State's Lance Palmer, 5–2, while Churella's father, Mark, the three-time NCAA champion, paced along the edge of the arena.

Gregor Gillespie and Head Coach Tim Flynn celebrate Gillespie's win in the 2007 NCAA 149-pound final.

Churella's opponent wouldn't be Schlatter, though. The Minnesota sophomore was losing to Gillespie 3–2, and as time expired, Gillespie turned to Flynn and Assistant Coach Cliff Moore and pumped both fists. One mountain had been scaled. One more awaited.

✦   ✦   ✦   ✦   ✦

O UTSIDE THE PALACE AT AUBURN HILLS, A LIGHT SNOW HAD coated the roads and parking lots overnight, and those who made their way to the arena on the afternoon of Saturday, March 17, 2007, found the going a little slower than usual.

It did nothing to hold down the crowd. Even with the finals televised live on ESPN, a record 17,780 fans filed into the Palace, a figure no doubt swelled by the intriguing possibility of seeing Josh Churella claim a national title in his home state.

Underneath the arena, in a concourse well away from the floor, Gregor Gillespie, wearing a large set of headphones he borrowed from his brother, was blocking out everything—the crowd, the hype surrounding Churella's pursuit of the hometown dream, the nerves that made his stomach pulse as he waited out his first national final.

Gillespie thought back to the training he had done in the basement at McComb Fieldhouse, lugging around buckets of concrete while Flynn and Rosselli, and later Flynn and Cliff Moore, barked at him and the rest of the Scots, reminding them that the only way they would get the respect of the rest of the country was to earn it.

He thought about the mind games that Flynn had played by calling his cell phone, pretending to be Dustin Schlatter. He thought about Minnesota coach J Robinson, a Gable disciple, and he convinced himself that Robinson never would have believed that Gillespie, coming out of high school, had the horsepower to beat Schlatter.

"I think we're a little more raw than most teams, a little more hungry," Gillespie recalled months later. "We go out in the grass and do buddy carries and put weights in Gatorade jugs and carry them all over campus. We flip a three hundred–pound tractor tire across the room. We get on our hands and knees and slide one hundred–pound weight plates up the hall. I think a lot of our guys look back at the training we do and think, 'Damn right I'm going to win this match.'"

That was the thought he carried with him when he saw Flynn running into the tunnel holding two red plastic bands for Gillespie

Gregor Gillespie celebrates his championship.

to strap to his ankles.

Once out in the arena, with the big crowd roaring, Gillespie shot right away, getting in on Churella's legs. Churella was able to fight him off and wait for a stalemate. The rest of regulation settled to a slower pace, and the match went to overtime tied 1–1. In the one-minute sudden victory, Churella took a deep shot that sent Gillespie's hips to the mat, but the referee, Dave Hickson, held off on making a quick takedown call, allowing Gillespie to work his way out from under Churella and to the side, where he reached for Churella's near leg. Gillespie had been in that same situation countless times in the practice room and during matches. Dangerous as it might have looked, close as Churella might have felt he was to securing the winning takedown, Gillespie believed he was in control.

"A lot of people who watched that match thought I was in a compromised position on his shot, but I'm actually pretty comfortable in that situation," Gillespie said. "As soon as I scooted out and grabbed his ankle, I looked at the ref and waited. I knew I was getting two points."

Hickson started in, and as Gillespie slipped behind a stunned Churella, the referee raised his arm, the one with the red wristband, and extended two fingers. The match was over. The Michigan fans were stunned. Gillespie was a Division I national champion, Edinboro's third and the program's youngest, having won it as a true sophomore. He hurled himself at his coaches, then turned to the small pocket of Edinboro fans in one corner of the arena and pointed in appreciation.

Gillespie hadn't exactly studied the program's history, but in the days that followed he knew what the win meant. He knew his wall chart from the nationals—the one showing his wins over four straight seeded wrestlers, including the Nos. 1 and 3 seeds from two powerhouse programs—would go into a frame and up on the wall in the basement of McComb Fieldhouse. He knew his oversized photo would go up in the wrestling office beside those the coaches had hung of Koscheck and O'Day, not far from the spot where DeAnna and Baumgartner, Jim McDonald's hand-picked disciples, had sat at that broken table and made the calls that helped bring together the pieces of Edinboro's first Division I squad.

He knew, as Koscheck and O'Day and Furey and Hahesy and all the others had known, that the battle for respect was far from over. The following season it would begin all over again. As long as there were overachieving Edinboros going up against Michigans and Iowas, the battle would never really end.

| Appendix |

All-Time Roster

A

Ace, Cory '98-03
Allen, Jay '92-93
Anderson, Barry '90-93
Andrassy, Joe '88-90
Armagost, Jim '94-95
Ashby, Michael '01-06
Atienza, Audie '89-90
Augustino, Paul '84-85

B

Bala, Chris '00-01, '02-05
Bartkowski, Anthony '89-90
Barton, Adam '88-89
Bartsh, Ed '85-86
Bauer, Ken '90-94
Bauer, Shawn '90-91
Bishoff, Clarence '88-89
Bockmore, Joe '05-07
Boe, Tim '03-04
Boozer, Ben '96-01
Bradshaw, Pat '05-07
Brewster, Casey '99-00
Brown, Chris '84-85
Bruns, Nick '85-89
Bubar, Dave '01-04
Bubnowski, Ron '95-97

Bunch, Shawn '01-06
Bundy, Nathan '99-01
Burger, Paul '04-06
Burklund, Brad '84-85
Buzas, Martin '88-89

C

Camino, Matt '00-02
Capriotti, John '90-91
Carls, Jim '87-89
Caros, Chad '98-02
Carpenito, Rob '85-86
Casey, Brendan '05-06
Cervone, Jeff '95-96
Chelsted, Matt '03-07
Christensen, Craig '85-88
Christensen, Erik '85-87
Chupak, Mike '85-88
Clark, Jody '92-93
Clark, Ken '98-00
Clemsen, Alex '02-07
Cocozzo, Daryl '06-07
Cook, Ryan '96-98
Cornelius, Larry '98-99
Courts, Vinnie '01-03
Cowden, B.C. '94-95
Coyle, B.J. '95-96
Crain, John '88-90

Cridge, Bruce '96-98
Cross, Jamie '06-07
Cubarney, Brian '90-92
Czarnecki, Ed '97-98

D

Daniels, Reuben '00-03
Daubert, Joe '89-90
Davia, Koel '04-05
Deel, John '87-88
DeForest, Eric '89-90
DelGarbino, John '92-93
Deubel, Ricky '04-07
Diamond, Dean '96-00
Davia, Koel '04-06
Davis, Ezra '05-06
Diamond, Yanni '98-01
Dilts, Kevin '88-90
DiMarco, Marc '89-91
DiPietro, Anthony '03-04
Doppelheuer, Ron '02-05

E

Evans, Josh '00-01

F

Feckanin, Steve '92-97
Felt, Steven '90-91
Fendone, Joe '04-07
Fendone, Shawn '06-07
Ferrara, C.J. '05-06
Fichter, Shane '94-95
Fiflet, Brad '00-03
Flanders, Robert '89-90

Fluke, Kyle '06-07
Flynn, Mike '84-89
Foley, John '06-07
Ford, Todd '96-98
Friburger, Bill '89-93
Fuller, Chris '94-98
Furey, Matt '84-86

G

Gabrielson, Jason '97-00
Galvan, Galo '92-93
Gear, Brian '88-92
Geibel, Donnie '03-04
Gibson, Jim '02-07
Gillespie, Gregor '05-07
Gilman, Kyle '93-94
Golden, Chris '90-91
Gray, Chip '84-85
Gray, Jacob '00-05
Green, Terry '88-91
Greene, Stan '97, '00-01
Gregan, Tom '87-88
Groenendaal, Eric '84-88
Gross, Eric '92-95

H

Hahesy, Mike '84-86
Hall, Dean '85-89
Happel, Dean '84-87
Harrison, Hayden '04-05
Hartman, Bert '90-91
Hawkins, Bill '93-95
Held, Dave '84-89
Held, Mike '86-90
Hennis, Joe '01-05

Hickman, Eric   '99-00
Hill, Matt   '02-07
Hiner, Kory   '06-07
Hjerling, Rob   '88-90
Hogue, Rick   '98-99
Hooks, Chamie   '97-98
Howard, Patrick   '98-00
Hudson, Mark   '02-03
Hunt, Rusty   '04-05
Hunt, Brian   '92-95

I

Imperator, Michael   '89-90

J

Johnson, A.J.   '95-00
Johnson, Erik   '85-88
Jones, Toussaint   '88-89
Joseph, Stephen   '99-00

K

Kaczor, Jim   '89-90
Kaday, Todd   '91-93
Karpowich, Ethan   '91, '95
Kauffman, Bob   '85-86
Keeney, Jamie   '96-97
Kegarise, Mike   '89-90
Kennedy, Terry   '84-89
Kibler, Ryan   '88-89
Kilburn, Korey   '94-99
Kim, Matt   '95-96
King, Matt D.   '01-04
King, Matt R.   '99-03
Knott, James   '90-91
Koscheck, Josh   '97-02

Kostman, Adam   '02-03

L

LaBella, Mike   '03-07
Lamoreaux, Matt   '86-90
Langfit, Dale   '88-91
Lautzenheiser, Cyle   '86-88
Lawrence, Bill   '93-97
Leone, Mike   '97-98
Linderson, Ryan   '98-99
Little, Jason   '98-99
Loukides, Jason   '89-94

M

Maher, Brian   '98-99
Mahoney, Scott   '89-91
Maier, Kevin   '98-00
Marcelli, Thad   '90-95
Marrs, Eddie   '91-93
Mazzerle, Larry   '97-98
McAlister, Seth   '04-06
McCormick, Heath   '93-94
McCormick, Tony   '87-88
McKay, Eric   '91-93
McLaughlin, Rick   '02-07
McQuiston, Dan   '92-96
Metz, Dave   '90-91
Midkiff, Bryan   '88-92
Mihalko, Shane   '02-04
Millard, Justin   '00-01
Miller, Allen   '86-87
Miller, Joe   '93-96
Minadeo, Randy   '87-88
Mitchell, Pete   '85-86
Montedoro, Chuck   '85-87

Moore, John   '97-98
Morello, John   '92-95
Moricone, Phil   '04-07
Morgan Ryan   '04-07
Morrill, Eric   '06-07
Morrison, Jay   '04-06
Mosley, Jeremy   '03-07
Moyers, Phil   '90-91
Mulligan, Jim   '89-90
Mumbulo, Nate   '02-04
Murdy, Chuck   '95-96
Murray, Craig   '93-97
Mussleman, Rich   '88-90
Myers, Frank   '85-86

O

O'Day, Sean   '85-89
O'Keefe, Tim   '93-95
Olszewski, Tom   '95-98
O'Meara, Kevin   '97-01
Orlandi, Kevin   '06-07
Osman, Mohamed   '04-06

P

Passoff, Mike   '89-91
Patrick, David   '00-01
Pearce, Josh   '97-02
Pedockie, Nick   '90-93
Penn, Deonte   '02-07
Peters, Mike   '86-87
Plerhoples, Zach   '02-07
Porter, Brett   '87-92
Porter, Rob   '84-89
Pruden, Chris   '03-04

R

Rapp, Josh   '96-97
Rawlins, Ed   '84-85
Ray, David   '85-86
Reed, Justin   '95-98
Rinella, Tony   '95-98
Ring, Eric   '01-06
Robertson, Guy   '85-86
Robie, Tony   '92-97
Robison, Jason   '93-98
Roe, Miles   '94-96
Ross, Anthony   '88-89
Rosselli, Lou   '88-93
Rowan, Dave   '84-88
Rutan, Dennis   '90-91
Ryan, Dennis   '84-85

S

Sample, Glenn   '02-03
Samples, Mark   '94-99
Sanchez, Marco   '93-94
Saniga, Kevin   '93-98
Saxton, Ricky   '06-07
Schuster, Pat   '92-97
Schutte, Justin   '03-04
Scriven, Fred   '94-95
Shafer, Aaron   '94-95
Shapert, Ryan   '96-01
Shapert, Shaun   '96-01
Shifflet, Tom   '90-95
Shunamon, David   '99-03
Sill, Greg   '04-07
Sluyter, Jason   '94-97
Smith, Ryan   '00-01
Smith, Ted   '84-85